Current
CONTROVERSIES

P9-DOE-031

Prisons

DISCARD

DATE DUE

FEB 1 5 2010	
APR 1 0 2010	
NOV 3 0 2011	
NOV 0 7 2012	
NOV 0 6 2013	

BRODART, CO.   Cat. No. 23-221

Other Books in the Current Controversies Series

Aid to Africa

Alternative Therapies

Anger Management

Assisted Suicide

Carbon Offsets

Darfur

Family Violence

Guns and Violence

Homeland Security

Homeschooling

Importing from China

Issues in Adoption

Media Ethics

The Rights of Animals

Torture

Vaccines

Prisons

Sylvia Engdahl, Book Editor

GREENHAVEN PRESS
A part of Gale, Cengage Learning

GALE
CENGAGE Learning™

Detroit • New York • San Francisco • New Haven, Conn • Waterville, Maine • London

GALE
CENGAGE Learning

Christine Nasso, *Publisher*
Elizabeth Des Chenes, *Managing Editor*

© 2010 Greenhaven Press, a part of Gale, Cengage Learning

Gale and Greenhaven Press are registered trademarks used herein under license.

For more information, contact:
Greenhaven Press
27500 Drake Rd.
Farmington Hills, MI 48331-3535
Or you can visit our Internet site at gale.cengage.com

ALL RIGHTS RESERVED.
No part of this work covered by the copyright herein may be reproduced, transmitted, stored, or used in any form or by any means graphic, electronic, or mechanical, including but not limited to photocopying, recording, scanning, digitizing, taping, Web distribution, information networks, or information storage and retrieval systems, except as permitted under Section 107 or 108 of the 1976 United States Copyright Act, without the prior written permission of the publisher.

For product information and technology assistance, contact us at

Gale Customer Support, 1-800-877-4253
For permission to use material from this text or product, submit all requests online at
www.cengage.com/permissions

Further permissions questions can be emailed to permissionrequest@cengage.com

Articles in Greenhaven Press anthologies are often edited for length to meet page requirements. In addition, original titles of these works are changed to clearly present the main thesis and to explicitly indicate the author's opinion. Every effort is made to ensure that Greenhaven Press accurately reflects the original intent of the authors. Every effort has been made to trace the owners of copyrighted material.

Cover image copyright © Glenn R. McGlaughlin, 2009. Used under license from Shutterstock.com.

LIBRARY OF CONGRESS CATALOGING-IN-PUBLICATION DATA

Prisons / Sylvia Engdahl, book editor.
    p. cm. -- (Current controversies)
  Includes bibliographical references and index.
  ISBN-13: 978-0-7377-4460-6 (hardcover)
  ISBN-13: 978-0-7377-4461-3 (pbk.)
  1. Prisons--United States. 2. Prison administration--United States. I. Engdahl, Sylvia.
  HV9471.P7822 2009
  365'.973--dc22

                                              2009024277

Printed in the United States of America
1 2 3 4 5 6 7 13 12 11 10 09

ACC LIBRARY SERVICES
AUSTIN, TX

Contents

Foreword   **13**

Introduction   **16**

Chapter 1: Are Too Many People Being Sent to Prison?

Chapter Preface   **22**

Yes: America's High Incarceration Rate Does Not Prevent Crime

Prisons Neither Deter Crime   **25**
Nor Rehabilitate Criminals

    Claire Gordon

    America imprisons more of its citizens than any other country, but only a small minority of inmates have committed violent crimes. Prison conditions are inhumane and perpetuate more violence.

Laws Mandating Longer Prison Sentences   **29**
Do Not Reduce Crime

    Steve Fennessy

    Prisons are overcrowded, and some states are recognizing that the traditional American model of corrections is not effective. There should be more emphasis on preparing criminals to hold jobs.

The Prison System Fails to Turn Criminals   **34**
Back into Citizens

    Jennifer Gonnerman

    America's prison system is becoming too expensive to sustain, in part because sentences, which are longer than sentences in other countries, are based on punishment and revenge rather than on rehabilitation.

Prison Expansion Is Not Cost-Effective   39
Michael Jacobson

States that increased incarceration during the 1990s had smaller declines in crime than other states. Research does not show that prison growth is justified on the basis of crime prevention.

No: Sending Criminals to Prison Is an Effective Means of Crime Prevention

A High Risk of Punishment Reduces Crime   44
George Will

Crime has become a less controversial political issue than it was a decade ago because Americans have been safer since the incarceration rate rose. Despite claims that the incarceration rate is too high, evidence shows that deterrence works.

Long Sentences for Repeat Offenders   47
Lower the Crime Rate
Debra J. Saunders

California's "Three Strikes" law, which mandates a twenty-five-year sentence for the third offense for criminals who have already committed two serious or violent felonies, is often criticized. The law, however, has caused the state's crime rate to fall dramatically.

The Cost of Leaving Criminals Loose   53
Exceeds the Cost of Prisons
Thomas Sowell

The cost of prisons seems high because it must be paid from government budgets, but the cost of letting criminals loose in society is paid by the public both in money and in being subjected to violence. Moreover, crime statistics are manipulated by advocates of alternatives to prisons.

Chapter 2: Are Inmates' Constitutional Rights Disregarded in American Prisons?

Chapter Preface   57

**Yes: The Conditions in Prisons Violate
Inmates' Constitutional Rights**

The Reproductive Rights of Women   59
in Prison Are Routinely Ignored
Rachel Roth

Women in prison are denied the right to make choices—
even choices about life-altering matters, such as major
surgery or continuing a pregnancy. Their medical needs
during pregnancy often are unmet, and those who have
children in foster care outside often lose parental rights
to them.

Male Rape in Prison Is Still Not   65
Taken Seriously
Dan Bell

Male rape, often accompanied by extreme violence, is
widespread in prisons. All too frequently the public jokes
about it, although victims often suffer long-term effects.
Congress passed the Prison Rape Elimination Act
(PREA), but so far it has done little good.

Female Prison Inmates Are Sexually   73
Assaulted by Guards
Jeff Seidel

In some prisons female prisoners have been raped or
molested by male guards. Lawsuits allege that state officials knew about it and did nothing; if many of these
suits are won, taxpayers may face hundreds of millions of
dollars in damages.

Minority Religions Are Not   **82**
Accommodated by Prison Policies

Bob Ritter

Although Congress passed the Religious Freedom Restoration Act (RFRA) in 1993, prison administrators and staff tend to view all religious observances from the perspective of the dominant faith, denying minority religions the opportunity to practice their own faith in its traditional manner.

Absent Physical Injury, Prison Abuse   **86**
Victims Cannot Sue in Federal Courts

Stephen B. Bright

People were horrified by prisoner abuse at Abu Ghraib in Iraq, but they do not realize that when comparable abuse occurs in prisons in this country, the law does not allow the victims to sue for damages in federal courts unless they can show evidence of physical injury.

**No: Conditions to Which Inmates Object
Are Not Always Unconstitutional**

Medical Care for Prison Inmates   **89**
Has Been Improved

Mark Taylor

Although in the past lack of medical care for prisoners has sometimes been ruled unconstitutional, court rulings have led to improvement. There are still many problems, especially in view of prison overcrowding, but efforts are being made to provide as much care as budgets allow.

Prison Inmates Will No Longer   **98**
Be Segregated by Race

Tanya Schevitz

After a prisoner filed suit on grounds that segregation violated his rights, the Supreme Court ruled that double cells in prisons must be desegregated. However, because many prisoners prefer to associate with their own race, forcing members of different races to share cells may cause trouble.

The Constitution Does Not Prohibit Serving   **103**
Prisoners Unappetizing Food

Arin Greenwood

In many prisons, inmates who misbehave are given Nutraloaf, which is nutritious but unappetizing, instead of regular food. Some inmates have sued, claiming this is a violation of their rights, but a group of lawyers who tasted Nutraloaf did not consider it unconstitutionally bad.

Imprisonment Is Not Supposed   **108**
To Be Enjoyable

James H. Lilley

Sheriff Joe Arpaio is well-known for the way he runs his jail, which he believes should not be a pleasant place for criminals. Although inmates complain, his methods—which include making them wear pink underwear—are successful in decreasing recidivism and should be copied elsewhere.

Chapter 3: What Can Be Done About Prison Overcrowding?

Chapter Preface   **115**

Many States Are Releasing Prisoners Early   **117**

Keith B. Richburg and Ashley Surdin

Because of overcrowded prisons and budget pressures, prisoners are being released early or placed on parole in many states. Such actions often are opposed by law enforcement officials and victims' groups, who fear that the public will be endangered or that justice will not be done.

A Federal Court May Rule that California's   **122**
Prison Population Must Be Reduced

Don Thompson

Federal judges are considering whether substandard conditions in California prisons are due solely to overcrowding. If they determine this is the case, the court may order early release of nearly 50,000 inmates, even though this would pose a risk to public safety.

Private Prisons Increase Capacity, Save   **126**
Money, and Improve Services

Nathan A. Benefield

Private prisons cost less, and evidence from thirty-four states shows they outperform state-run institutions on quality and performance indicators. Moreover, in the private sector, prison managers and staff are held accountable for mismanagement; a company that fails to perform will go out of business.

Private Prisons Can Ease Overcrowding   **133**
But May Be Flawed

William Bender

Opinions differ about whether private prisons are successful. Critics say prison companies cut corners to increase profits and do not provide adequate services to inmates. Some states are expanding their use of privatization, but labor union opposition has prevented expansion in other states.

Some States May House Prisoners in Tents   **140**

Richard Luscombe

In Florida, giant tents are being set up in case they are needed to avoid prison overcrowding, but some people believe Florida's climate will make them intolerably hot. There and in other states, tents have been used in the past for short-term housing, and their permanent use is being considered.

Electronic Monitoring May Be an Effective   **144**
Alternative to Prison

Dana DiFilippo

In some jurisdictions nonviolent criminals are monitored electronically instead of being locked up. New monitoring systems have global positioning system (GPS) capability to track offenders' movements.

Chapter 4: How Are Recent Trends Affecting Prisons?

Chapter Preface   **148**

Cell Phones Are a Growing Threat   **150**
to Prison Security
Robert K. Gordon

Cell phones are banned in prisons because inmates often
use them to arrange outside crimes, but prisoners find
many ways to smuggle them in and hide them. Prison
administrators want to jam cell phone reception, but because jamming phones is against federal law, they cannot
yet do so.

The Prison Population Is Aging   **155**
Carrie Abner

Elderly inmates represent the fastest growing segment of
the prison population because of mandatory sentencing
laws and because inmates are living longer. Inmates also
develop age-related health problems earlier than average,
and the financial burden of caring for them is increasing.

Many States Have Eliminated Parole   **164**
Jens Soering

Many states have abolished parole under "truth in sentencing" laws, legislation that is profitable for the prison
industry. The parole system rewards prisoners for good
behavior; however, inmates who have no prospect of parole, especially those with life sentences, have no incentive to better themselves.

Prison Camps Can No Longer Be Dismissed   **173**
as "Country Clubs"
Luke Mullins

Living conditions in federal prison camps used to be
relatively pleasant, but in recent years camps have become more like higher-security prisons and no longer offer inmates as many privileges. The white-collar criminals who once populated such camps are now
outnumbered by drug offenders.

More Criminals Are Being Sent   **183**
to Supermax Prisons
Jeffrey Ian Ross

The number of Supermax prisons, designed to house the
most violent, hardened, and escape-prone criminals, has
been growing. Known for their strict lockdown policies,
lack of amenities, and prisoner isolation techniques, Supermax prisons are increasingly used for gang leaders, serial killers, and terrorists.

Redesigned Prisons Provide Humane   **193**
Environments for Inmates
Richard Wener

Some newer prisons are designed very differently from
traditional ones; they are decentralized, with officers directly supervising specific living units. It is thought that
providing inmates with humane settings and expecting
civil behavior from them results in a better and safer environment.

Dog-Training Programs in Prisons Give   **200**
Inmates Second Chances
Matthew Schniper

Many prisons now have programs through which inmates are selected to train dogs rescued from shelters to
become companion or service animals. The inmates as
well as the dogs learn acceptable behavior from these
programs, and the inmates gain skills that enable them to
get jobs after release.

Organizations to Contact   **210**

Bibliography   **215**

Index   **221**

Foreword

By definition, controversies are "discussions of questions in which opposing opinions clash" (*Webster's Twentieth Century Dictionary Unabridged*). Few would deny that controversies are a pervasive part of the human condition and exist on virtually every level of human enterprise. Controversies transpire between individuals and among groups, within nations and between nations. Controversies supply the grist necessary for progress by providing challenges and challengers to the status quo. They also create atmospheres where strife and warfare can flourish. A world without controversies would be a peaceful world; but it also would be, by and large, static and prosaic.

The Series' Purpose

The purpose of the *Current Controversies* series is to explore many of the social, political, and economic controversies dominating the national and international scenes today. Titles selected for inclusion in the series are highly focused and specific. For example, from the larger category of criminal justice, *Current Controversies* deals with specific topics such as police brutality, gun control, white collar crime, and others. The debates in *Current Controversies* also are presented in a useful, timeless fashion. Articles and book excerpts included in each title are selected if they contribute valuable, long-range ideas to the overall debate. And wherever possible, current information is enhanced with historical documents and other relevant materials. Thus, while individual titles are current in focus, every effort is made to ensure that they will not become quickly outdated. Books in the *Current Controversies* series will remain important resources for librarians, teachers, and students for many years.

In addition to keeping the titles focused and specific, great care is taken in the editorial format of each book in the series. Book introductions and chapter prefaces are offered to provide background material for readers. Chapters are organized around several key questions that are answered with diverse opinions representing all points on the political spectrum. Materials in each chapter include opinions in which authors clearly disagree as well as alternative opinions in which authors may agree on a broader issue but disagree on the possible solutions. In this way, the content of each volume in *Current Controversies* mirrors the mosaic of opinions encountered in society. Readers will quickly realize that there are many viable answers to these complex issues. By questioning each author's conclusions, students and casual readers can begin to develop the critical thinking skills so important to evaluating opinionated material.

Current Controversies is also ideal for controlled research. Each anthology in the series is composed of primary sources taken from a wide gamut of informational categories including periodicals, newspapers, books, U.S. and foreign government documents, and the publications of private and public organizations. Readers will find factual support for reports, debates, and research papers covering all areas of important issues. In addition, an annotated table of contents, an index, a book and periodical bibliography, and a list of organizations to contact are included in each book to expedite further research.

Perhaps more than ever before in history, people are confronted with diverse and contradictory information. During the Persian Gulf War, for example, the public was not only treated to minute-to-minute coverage of the war, it was also inundated with critiques of the coverage and countless analyses of the factors motivating U.S. involvement. Being able to sort through the plethora of opinions accompanying today's major issues, and to draw one's own conclusions, can be a complicated and frustrating struggle. It is the editors' hope that *Current Controversies* will help readers with this struggle.

Introduction

Although captivity in various forms has been common throughout human history, incarceration as a judicially imposed sentence for crime is a comparatively recent development. Until after the American revolution, people who committed serious crimes were generally executed, while lesser offenders received corporal punishment such as whipping or being placed in the stocks. Offenders generally were held in jail—usually under appalling conditions—only before trial or while waiting for their sentences to be carried out. Long-term imprisonment was reserved for political prisoners and debtors.

The first U.S. state prisons were built in the late eighteenth and early nineteenth centuries. In the beginning their aim was to reform the inmates, mainly by harsh methods that today seem cruel and counterproductive. They were called penitentiaries because criminals were expected to repent and do penance. Prison reformers, having seen that the squalor and crowding of traditional jails led to violence among the inmates, starvation, and disease, went to the opposite extreme. They introduced extreme regimentation, hard labor, and isolation of inmates from each other.

The most famous of these early prisons was Eastern State Penitentiary in Philadelphia, opened in 1829, which was the worldwide model for what became known as the Pennsylvania System. In the physical sense it was vastly superior to its predecessors: an imposing fortress with seven wings of cellblocks radiating from a central hub that was, and still is, a prominent tourist attraction. As Chai Woodham wrote in a recent *Smithsonian.com* article, "With central heating, flush toilets, and shower baths in each private cell, the penitentiary boasted luxuries that not even President Andrew Jackson could enjoy at the White House."

However, these amenities were not provided for the prisoners' comfort. Under the Pennsylvania System, inmates were kept in permanent solitary confinement. They were hooded during entry to the prison and never saw any of it beyond their individual cells; guards observed and communicated with them only through small feeding holes. The designers believed that if convicts were forced to confront their crimes in isolation from others, they would find peace through penitence, so that upon release they could leave their unsavory past lives behind. But not everyone agreed with this theory. Novelist Charles Dickens was horrified by what he saw, and in *American Notes* he wrote, "I am persuaded that those who designed this system . . . do not know what it is they are doing . . . I hold the slow and daily tampering with the mysteries of the brain to be immeasurably worse than any torture of the body."

Eastern State's system of total isolation was abandoned in 1913, not only because it had been shown not to work but because of overcrowding. The prison had been designed for 300 inmates but by the 1920s it held more than 2,000 in shared cells, including new ones built below ground without windows or plumbing. After decades of deterioration Eastern State was closed in 1971. Long before that time, reformation had ceased to be the focus of prisons, and punishment had come to be seen as their main purpose. Corruption and abuse were prevalent, despite a movement toward reform in the late nineteenth century that resulted in such innovations as inmate education, rewards for good behavior, and parole.

Reformers were particularly opposed to the contract labor system, under which inmates were leased under contract to private companies that sold the products of their work and split the profits with the state. This was considered unfair competition by businesses and labor unions, and so in 1887 Congress prohibited the use of federal prisoners for contract labor. Because the states then became unwilling to house federal prisoners, the first federal prisons were established. Some of the states also passed laws prohibiting contract labor, and gradually it was replaced by a system under which prisoners worked directly for the states, for example, by producing license plates or building roads. From the prisoners' standpoint this brought little improvement, especially in the South where the roadwork was done by chain gangs whose members were treated like slaves and received brutal physical punishment at the slightest sign of disobedience. The chain gangs were abolished in the late 1930s, both because of public protests and because during the Depression it was felt prisoners should not be doing work that could be done by free laborers who needed jobs.

In the mid-twentieth century the civil rights movement led to more sympathy for prisoners, fueled by the increasing incarceration of African Americans. Prisoners' rights began to receive attention, and a series of court decisions gave inmates access to the courts, which had previously been denied them. Belief that criminals could become constructive citizens through education increased, and in some states great emphasis was placed on the rehabilitative aspect of imprisonment. Prisoners became involved in political activism, accompanied by publicity provided by activists on the outside. The public began to perceive them as victims, or in a few cases, even as heroes.

But these developments soon backfired. There were a number of bloody prison riots, which led to a large increase in federal and state funding for heightened security and discipline. Reaction against the radical political element, which viewed imprisonment as unjustifiable oppression, began to overshadow the efforts of more moderate groups working to improve the condition of prisoners. At the same time, a victims' rights movement was growing. It was widely believed that the best way to help victims of crime was to punish criminals more severely, although whether this really serves victims' needs is controversial. The women's rights movement, which sensitized the public to the issue of rape and other violence against women, also contributed to the trend toward getting tougher on all crime. By the late twentieth century this trend had become dominant. There are more than five times as many federal and state prisoners in 2009 as there were thirty years ago, and the majority of them are in prisons where little attention is paid to efforts toward rehabilitation.

Today, prisons vary widely in how inmates are housed and the way they are treated. Most are "standard" medium-security prisons where the inmates share small cells on corridors patrolled by guards and are allowed to mingle for meals and exercise. Some, however, provide more normal surroundings, even furniture and carpets, and officers are assigned to supervise specific living units. There also are minimum-security camps where inmates live in barracks. At the other extreme, in Supermax prisons used only for the worst offenders, the round-the-clock solitary confinement so appalling to Charles Dickens is now back. All of these arrangements have both advocates and opponents. Increasingly, funding problems and overcrowding make it impossible to achieve a balance that anyone considers satisfactory.

Is the purpose of prison to punish the criminal, to rehabilitate, to deter others from crime, or simply to protect the public from individuals who are dangerous? Opinions vary widely about this. It is generally conceded, even by strong opponents of imprisonment, that it is necessary for violent repeat offenders to be locked up. On the other hand, whether prisons have any deterrent value is a hotly debated issue. Another strongly debated issue is the effectiveness of rehabilitation efforts, considering that more than two-thirds of the convicts released are rearrested for new crimes within three years and more than half are returned to prison. Many experts believe criminals could be rehabilitated more effectively through community-based programs such as electronic monitoring, while others feel that this is unlikely.

The question of punishment is probably the one most fundamental to the prison debate. It is obvious that crime must have consequences—if it did not, there would be no respect for the law, and the public would be at the mercy of whoever chose to ignore it. Punishment for its own sake is another matter. Many people believe that criminals deserve to be punished and made to suffer not merely to discourage repetition of their acts, in the sense that children are punished so that they will learn to behave, but because crime is an offense against morality. Others believe that it is not right for society to pass judgment on people except insofar as is necessary to protect the innocent. These two positions are not always articulated, but they are integral to the differing views of who should be sent to prison and what should happen to prisoners while they are there.

CHAPTER 1

Are Too Many People Being Sent to Prison?

Chapter Preface

The Pew Center on the States, a nonprofit research organization, released a landmark report in February 2008 on American prisons. The report was widely discussed in the media, and Pew issued a second report in March 2009. Both reports analyze extensive statistics on the nation's prisons, and these statistics have caused many people to react with dismay. They reveal that one in thirty-one American adults is under the control of the correctional system—in jail or prison, on probation, or on parole—and this does not count forms of supervision, such as special drug courts and alternative sentencing units, for which comprehensive data cannot be obtained. One in a hundred adults is behind bars in the United States, a much higher percentage of the population than is imprisoned in any other country. In fact, there are more prisoners in the United States than in China, a considerably larger and, many contend, more repressive nation. Moreover, the prison population is growing rapidly. And yet, according to the Pew reports, as this growth continues incarceration will cost more and have less impact on the crime rate than in the past.

"Americans deserve criminal justice policies that keep them safe. They want violent and chronic criminals to be put in prison. At the same time, a majority of Americans support cost-effective strategies for dealing with offenders who pose less risk to the community," Pew states on its Web site. This is true—but the questions of who to incarcerate and for how long are extremely controversial. Many people, especially social scientists and human rights activists, believe far too many offenders are imprisoned and that this high incarceration rate does not result in less crime. Others believe keeping criminals in prison for long periods does reduce crime and is essential to public safety. Since the 1980s, the public has increasingly demanded "tough on crime" policies, leading to the passage of mandatory minimum sentence laws and "three strikes" statutes that require people who commit a third felony to be given a twenty-five-year-to-life sentence for certain crimes.

This trend represents a change from earlier decades of the twentieth century, during which the concept of rehabilitation was on the rise. By the 1960s, imprisonment was generally viewed less as punishment than as a method by which prisoners could be reformed. But in the 1980s and 1990s the prevalence of crime became a major public issue, and politicians responded to the public's fear of crime and general belief that judges often were too lenient. The result was a decreased emphasis on rehabilitation and the imposition of sentences that caused rapid expansion of the prison population. Because this policy is now well established, less has been written to argue for it recently than in the past; arguments against current practices often are more prevalent than those in favor of them. It should not be thought, however, that majority opinion has swung away from the belief that locking up criminals is the best way to ensure public safety. On the contrary, voters continue to support the building of more prisons, and few government officials want to be considered soft on crime.

The common desire to reduce crime is not at issue, but the controversy concerns the most effective way to accomplish this goal. Critics of the present policy argue that nonviolent criminals, especially drug users, do not belong in prison and can be better dealt with through treatment and supervision within their communities. But some people maintain that even minor offenders should be punished in prison simply because they have broken the law. Others argue that minor offenders are potentially dangerous to the public whether or not they have yet committed violent crimes. There also is disagreement about whether incarceration of convicted criminals deters others from committing crimes. Some experts are convinced that it does, while opponents believe it has no significant deterrent effect.

As David Keene, president of the American Conservative Union, said to Pew researchers, "The fact that so many Americans, including hundreds of thousands who are a threat to no one, are incarcerated means that something is wrong with our criminal justice system and the way we deal with both dangerous criminals and those whose behavior we simply don't like." There seems to be a growing consensus that changes to the system are needed because the huge expense of imprisoning more and more people is consuming an ever-larger share of public funds. Even those who favor locking up as many offenders as possible may begin to see a time when the costs of operating more and more prisons simply cannot be sustained.

Prisons Neither Deter Crime Nor Rehabilitate Criminals

Claire Gordon

Claire Gordon is a student at Saybrook College at Yale University.

One in 100 American adults is behind bars. That's 2.3 million people total. America imprisons more of its citizens than any other country in the world. China runs a close second, but of course, China has four times as many people as the U.S. and is also a Communist dictatorship. America's incarceration rate is higher than every country in Europe combined. In fact, the prison population in the U.S. is equivalent to five Luxembourgs.

American prisons offer a grim portrait of our country's underclass. 1 in 36 Hispanic adults are currently incarcerated, as is one in nine black men aged 20 to 34. One in three black men will be imprisoned in his lifetime. Although illegal drug use is equally prevalent among white and black males, a black man is five times more likely to be arrested. A higher percentage of the black population is currently imprisoned in America than in South Africa at the height of apartheid.

When one percent of your population is housed, clothed, fed and supervised by the state, there's going to be an inevitably hefty price tag. It costs an average of $23,876 to imprison someone for a year in the United States. In Rhode Island it costs $45,000, the same as a year's worth of tuition, room and board at Brown University. Our own state of Connecticut spends as much money on its prisons as it does on higher education. In twenty years, average state spending on corrections has nearly quintupled to $49 billion. Although crime rates are dropping, this number continues to climb.

Claire Gordon, "Prisons Commit Greater Crime than Inmates," *Yale Daily News*. Copyright © 2002 Yale Daily News Publishing Company, Inc. All rights reserved. Reprinted with Permission.

And it isn't paying off. America has the highest homicide rate out of all industrialized nations. In the world ranking, Iraq is only three places ahead. The idea that the prison system makes us safer is based on two principles. The first is that the threat of incarceration deters crime in the first place. The second is that criminals are isolated from society and rehabilitated, so that on release they won't offend again. But the current prison system has failed to fulfill either of these postulates. Since the [19]80s, crime rates have fallen as incarceration rates have climbed. It is not the threat of arrest that has affected crime rates, but rather the economy, the rate of unemployment and drug use. In the 1990s, the states with the least rapidly rising incarceration rates actually experienced the most dramatic drops in crime.

America imprisons more of its citizens than any other country in the world.

Prisons also typically fail to rehabilitate. In fact, they actively do the opposite. Inmates are exploited for cheap labor and endure overcrowding, brutality and poor services. They don't cure criminal minds, but perpetuate violence. The United States increasingly builds its prisons as giant Supermax facilities—concrete and steel and stark efficiency. Inmates are often kept in solitary confinement for 23 hours a day and, thanks to new technology, have almost no interpersonal interactions. Advocates have long criticized these units as responsible for mental degeneration and derangement. The United Nations has denounced them as inhumane. A recent spate of lawsuits have claimed that Supermaxes violate the 8th Amendment ban on cruel and unusual punishment.

Although American prisons are financially and ethically grievous, the incarceration rate continues to skyrocket with hardly a peep from politicians. This may be because the prison system impacts our society's most disempowered. Once you're convicted of a felony, you are stripped of your rights as a citizen. (In seven states, a quarter of the entire black male population is permanently ineligible to vote.) The fact that the prison system acts as an often-privatized, productive growth industry for the country (the third largest) offers tangible economic benefits that keep politicians tight-lipped. After all, prisons need to be built, prisoners clothed, supervised and provided for. Looking for access to a 35 billion dollar industry, corporations, defense giants and investment banks are eager providers.

And so the prison-industrial complex is born: a conglomeration of special interests that encourages more and more spending. The prison-industrial complex demands constant and ever-increasing growth, even though this translates into more human lives in cages, more racist policing and more Supermax units. The same corporations that fuel the prison industry also fund politicians, to the tune of $33 million in 44 states in the 2002 and 2004 elections. It is therefore not so surprising then that the prison system has never been the top of the agenda for any liberal or conservative politician.

Prisoners may have broken the law, but our prisons, as they exist right now, are committing crimes against humanity.

It is often difficult for people to garner much sympathy for the victims of our prison system. In the popular imagination these people are vicious murderers, rapists and pedophiles. However, perpetrators of violent crime make up a vast minority of inmates and even the worst criminals are human beings, the majority of which have grown up in poverty and abusive households. The prison system is the way our society deals with the poor, drug-addicted, homeless and mentally ill. Sixty percent of inmates are illiterate. 60 to 80 percent have a history of substance abuse. Two hundred thousand suffer serious mental illness. In a Colorado Supermax, a quarter of the inmates are on anti-psychotic medication. When released, these people will experience restricted employment opportunities, often prohibited from getting federal loans or public housing. In this way, our prison system disenfranchises the already destitute.

The prison system needs to stop expanding in numbers; prisons need to de-politicize parole, courts need to repeal the three strikes policy and their draconian drug laws and our resources need to be concentrated on those already behind bars. At the moment, drug treatment is available to only one in ten inmates who need it, half the number it was in 1993. Prisons need to provide counseling, treatment programs, education, job training, expanded visiting rooms, family support and extended healthcare. Prisoners may have broken the law, but our prisons, as they exist right now, are committing crimes against humanity.

Laws Mandating Longer Prison Sentences Do Not Reduce Crime

Steve Fennessy

Steve Fennessy is the deputy editor of Atlanta Magazine.

G eorgia's politicians may disagree about a lot of things, but they find remarkable unanimity when it comes to locking up criminals. This is probably no surprise; passing laws that put convicts behind bars for longer and longer stretches offends no one, except maybe the criminals themselves and judges who don't like being told how to do their jobs.

But Georgia's ambitious sense of justice extends beyond just violent criminals. Eight years ago, almost half of state prison inmates were behind bars on nonviolent offenses, such as forgery or cocaine possession. Today, that percentage has barely budged. The result? Our prisons are bursting. In the past ten years, the state population grew by 24 percent, while the number of state prisoners expanded at twice that rate. For every dollar spent on higher education, we spend fifty cents housing prisoners. Georgia, in fact, imprisons more of its residents than does all of Algeria, a country that has almost four times our population and is hardly a slouch when it comes to meting out justice.

The problem is not unique to Georgia. Earlier this year, research by the Pew Center on the States concluded that the U.S. had crossed a "sobering threshold: for the first time, more than one in every 100 adults is now confined in an American jail or prison." But even within this context, Georgia is exceptional, and not in a good way. Not only do we have an over-developed sense of vengeance (last year, one out of every

Steve Fennessy, "Over-corrections," *Atlanta Magazine*, vol. 48, October 2008, pp. 46, 48, 50. Copyright © 2008 Atlanta Magazine. All rights reserved. Reproduced by permission.

seventy-seven adults in Georgia was behind bars), but other states are recognizing that the traditional American model of corrections is broken and are taking measures to fix it.

Statutes like the "two strikes" law produced unintended consequences.

Will Georgia do the same?

Tough Minimum Sentencing Laws

In 1994, under then-Governor Zell Miller, Georgia voters approved the toughest minimum sentencing laws in the nation, sometimes known as "two strikes"—ten years with no parole for a first violent offense, such as rape or kidnapping, life without parole for a second. Around the same time, the state's Board of Pardons and Paroles, which had traditionally acted as a release valve to keep prison populations in check, tightened its parole policy. Last year [2007], for example, the board granted an early release to 12,054 inmates, almost the same number as it did in 1993. Which would be fine, if the prison population had stayed the same. Only it didn't. It doubled.

The combination of mandatory minimums and a stricter parole board sent Georgia's prison population soaring. When James Donald took over as state prisons chief in 2003, the methamphetamine scourge was spreading fast. Today, Donald says, the prison system takes in up to 300 meth addicts a month, putting an even greater strain on the system.

Donald is Georgia's first African American corrections commissioner. A Mississippi native, he first met Governor Sonny Perdue in 2003 at a memorial service for soldiers killed in Iraq. At the time, Donald was a two-star Army general with no experience in corrections. He had a comfortable retirement to look forward to, but when Perdue asked him to take the prison job, he accepted. "It's not about the money," he says. "It's about making a difference."

When it comes to overcrowding, a corrections commissioner's options are limited. In Donald's case, he saw that statutes like the "two strikes" law produced unintended consequences. By forcing an offender to serve ten years with no chance at parole, hundreds of violent criminals sentenced in the early days of the law were being let out after ten years. And there often was no oversight of them because they had maxed out their sentences. "Supervision of an inmate when he gets out fundamentally may be more important than how long you lock him up," Donald says.

One of the tools Donald does have at his disposal is the bully pulpit. In speeches to Rotary groups and churches, he has stressed the need to distinguish between prisoners we're afraid of and those we're simply mad at. It's a savvy bit of marketing that serves dual purposes: assuaging the law-and-order crowd while also acknowledging—gently—that the status quo is not a viable model for the future.

A shrinking prison population does not necessarily mean higher crime rates.

"We're a law-and-order state, but we can use good, prudent common sense," he says. Some of his common-sense solutions? More day reporting centers, in which nonviolent drug offenders serve their sentences in the community, but where they must check in daily for a drug test and undergo intensive counseling. In this way, the offender can live at home, hold a job, and support his family. Currently there are six such centers throughout the state, and Donald estimates they're keeping a thousand felons a year from joining the general prison population. It costs taxpayers $14 a day to monitor a convict this way, compared with $47 a day if he or she is in a state prison.

"This is a much more effective technique," Donald says. "I can keep 'em locked up for five or six years, but if they come home and haven't learned to deal with their addictions, they'll still have the motivation [to commit a crime]. This is having great success."

Get Donald talking and he's hard to stop. Besides the reporting centers, he talks about the need for more work-release programs, halfway houses, and alliances between corporations and prisons to groom promising convicts for work once they're released.

"Fifty-one percent of our [prison] population has never held a job," Donald says. "What I've found is that work is a learned behavior. When Daddy put that wagon out on the cotton field when I was a little boy in the 1950s, I knew what that meant. So many people have an expectation to be given things all their lives, and that has created a lot of pressure on society."

Lowering the Crime Rate

When a criminal is in jail, he's not out on the street committing crimes. So it's logical to conclude that as prison populations go up, crime rates should come down. And in fact, as Georgia began locking up more and more criminals, violent crime went down by 44 percent. The rate of murders fell by half.

The length of a possible prison sentence doesn't deter a would-be criminal as much as the certainty that he'll be caught and swiftly punished.

But that theory doesn't always hold true. In the 1980s, the number of inmates in Georgia prisons almost doubled. But crime skyrocketed, peaking in 1990 when there were eight violent crimes—things like rape, murder, and shootings—for every thousand people in the state. (In 2006, that number had fallen to four.)

Conversely, a shrinking prison population does not necessarily mean higher crime rates. New York has had fewer state inmates every year since 1999, and yet its crime rate continues to drop. The state has put more prisoners into shock camps, where they serve shorter sentences and even earn GEDs. Recidivism rates have fallen.

What's the answer? No one knows for sure. One theory is that the length of a possible prison sentence doesn't deter a would-be criminal as much as the certainty that he'll be caught and swiftly punished. If that's true, clearing out backlogged court dockets and giving more resources to police departments to deal with criminals are more important than the length of the sentence. Criminal careers don't often last past middle age, it seems.

"Most people who commit crimes age out, to some extent," says Stephen B. Bright, president and senior counsel of the Southern Center for Human Rights, which represents indigent clients and the wrongfully convicted and argues for better conditions in jails throughout the South. "When you're eighteen to twenty-four, there's a lot of testosterone, no education, no hope. They're involved in drugs and robbing people and they're a real menace to society. But a lot of those people, when they get to be thirty-five to forty, they've matured and they're different people."

To Bright, the root of the problem lies in schools. "We have this system where there are a lot of children who are growing up who are not getting education, opportunity, and hope. If you don't have those three things, you're going to have a failure. What this speaks to is a failure of the public schools in Georgia. If you want to talk about crime, and the moral implications of this, it's about the failure of education."

The Prison System Fails to Turn Criminals Back into Citizens

Jennifer Gonnerman

Jennifer Gonnerman is a journalist who has written for many magazines. Her book Life on the Outside *was a finalist for the 2004 National Book Award.*

The number first appeared in headlines earlier this year: Nearly one in four of all prisoners worldwide is incarcerated in America. It was just the latest such statistic. Today, one in nine African American men between the ages of 20 and 34 is locked up. In 1970, our prisons held fewer than 200,000 people; now that number exceeds 1.5 million, and when you add in local jails, it's 2.3 million—1 in 100 American adults. Since the 1980s, we've sat by as the numbers inched higher and our prison system ballooned, swallowing up an ever-larger portion of the citizenry. But do statistics like these, no matter how disturbing, really mean anything anymore? What does it take to get us to sit up and notice?

Apparently, it takes a looming financial crisis. For there is another round of bad news, the logical extension of the first: The more money a state spends on building and running prisons, the less there is for everything else, from roads and bridges to health care and public schools. At the pace our inmate population has been expanding, America's prison system is becoming, quite simply, too expensive to sustain. That is why Kansas, Texas, and at least 11 other states have been trying out new strategies to curb the cost—reevaluating their parole policies, for instance, so that not every parolee who runs afoul of an administrative rule is shipped straight back to prison. And yet our infatuation with incarceration continues.

Jennifer Gonnerman, "Slammed," *Mother Jones*, July/August 2008. Copyright © 2008 Foundation for National Progress. Reproduced by permission.

There have been numerous academic studies and policy reports and journalistic accounts analyzing our prison boom, but this phenomenon cannot be fully measured in numbers. That much became apparent to me when, beginning in 2000, I spent nearly four years shadowing a woman who'd just been released from prison. She'd been locked up for 16 years for a first-time drug crime, and her absence had all but destroyed her family. Her mother had taken in her four young children after her arrest, only to die prematurely of kidney failure. One daughter was deeply depressed, the other was seething with rage, and her youngest son had followed her lead, diving into the neighborhood drug culture and then winding up in prison himself.

Nearly one in four of all prisoners worldwide is incarcerated in America.

The criminal justice system had punished not only her but her entire family. How do you measure the years of wasted hours—riding on a bus to a faraway prison, lining up to be scanned and searched and questioned, sitting in a bleak visiting room waiting for a loved one to walk in? How do you account for all the dollars spent on collect calls from prison— calls that can cost at least three times as much as on the outside because the prison system is taking a cut? How do you begin to calculate the lessons absorbed by children about deprivation and punishment and vengeance? How do you end the legacy of incarceration?

American Sentences Are Exceptionally Severe

This is not to say that nobody deserves to go to prison or that we should release everyone who is now locked up. There are many people behind bars who you would not want as your neighbor, but in our hunger for justice we have lost perspective. We treat 10-year sentences like they're nothing, like that's a soft penalty, when in much of the rest of the world a decade behind bars would be considered extraordinarily severe. This is what separates us from other industrialized countries: It's not just that we send so many people to prison, but that we keep them there for so long and send them back so often. Eight years ago, we surpassed Russia to claim the dubious distinction of having the world's highest rate of incarceration; today we're still No. 1.

America is expert at turning citizens into convicts, but we've forgotten how to transform convicts back into citizens.

If awards were granted to the country with the most surreal punishments, we would certainly win more than our share. Thirty-six straight years in solitary confinement (the fate of two men convicted in connection with the murder of a guard in Louisiana's Angola prison). A 55-year sentence for a small-time pot dealer who carried a gun during his sales (handed down by a federal court in Utah in 2004). Life sentences for 13-year-olds. (In 2005, Human Rights Watch counted more than 2,000 American inmates serving life without parole for crimes committed as juveniles. The entire rest of the world has only locked up 12 kids without hope of release.) Female prisoners forced to wear shackles while giving birth. (Amnesty International found 48 states that permitted this practice as of 2006.) A ban on former prisoners working as barbers (on the books in New York state).

America is expert at turning citizens into convicts, but we've forgotten how to transform convicts back into citizens. In 1994, Congress eliminated Pell grants for prisoners, a move that effectively abolished virtually all of the 350 prison college programs across the country. That might not seem like a catastrophe, until you consider that education has been *proven* to help reduce recidivism. (This was the conclusion of a recent paper by the Urban Institute, which reviewed 49 separate studies.) As the *New York Times'* Adam Liptak has pointed out, our prisons used to be models of redemption; [French political thinker and historian Alexis] de Tocqueville praised them in *Democracy in America.* Many prisons still call themselves "correctional facilities," but the term has become a misnomer. Most abandoned any pretense of rehabilitation long ago. Former California governor Jerry Brown even went so far as to rewrite the state's penal code to stress that the primary mission of that state's prisons is punishment.

There are many people behind bars who you would not want as your neighbor, but in our hunger for justice we have lost perspective.

Freed Prisoners Become Second-Class Citizens

Our cell blocks are packed with men and women who cannot read or write, who never graduated from high school—75 percent of state inmates—who will be hard-pressed to find a job once they are released. Once freed, they become second-class citizens. Depending on the state, they may be denied public housing, student loans, a driver's license, welfare benefits, and a wide range of jobs. Perhaps there is no more damning statistic than the fact that within three years, half will be convicted of a new crime.

Recently, there have been some hopeful signs. In April [2008], the Second Chance Act was finally signed into law; it will provide federal grants to programs that help prisoners reenter society. But our punishment industry—which each year spends millions lobbying federal and state lawmakers—has grown so massive and so entrenched that it will take far more than one piece of legislation to begin to undo its far-reaching effects.

Just look at our felony disenfranchisement laws, which prohibit 5.3 million people from voting—including 13 percent of African American men. These numbers actually underestimate the scope of the problem, as many ex-prisoners believe they cannot vote even if they can. And so the legacy of our prison boom continues: We've become a two-tier society in which millions of ostensibly free people are prohibited from enjoying the rights and privileges accorded to everyone else— and we continue to be defined by our desire for punishment and revenge, rather than by our belief in the power of redemption.

Prison Expansion
Is Not Cost-Effective

Michael Jacobson

Michael Jacobson is a former New York City corrections commissioner who is now director of the Vera Institute of Justice.

The United States now spends over $60 billion annually to maintain its corrections system reflecting the fact that we imprison a greater percentage of our population than any other nation on earth. In the last 30 years, we have seen the jail and prison population rise from 250 thousand to almost 2.3 million, almost a ten-fold increase.

The strain that this geometric increase in those incarcerated puts on our states and cities is cumulative and continues to grow. Over the last decade and a half, the only function of state governments to grow as a percentage of overall state budgets is, with the exception of Medicaid, corrections. The rate of growth of spending on corrections in state budgets exceeds that for education, health care, social services, transportation and environmental protection. There is a very clear relationship between the amount of money we spend on prisons and the amount that is available, or not available, for all these other essential areas of government. In many states—California is one that especially comes to mind—one can literally see money move in the budget from primary and secondary education to prisons. State budgets tend to be largely zero sum games and increases in corrections spending has absolutely held down spending in these other areas of government, many of which are also directly related to public safety.

Of course, the obvious question this raises is, "what do we get for that money?" Certainly, there should be some signifi-

Michael Jacobson, "Mass Incarceration in the United States: At What Cost?" *Testimony to a hearing of the Senate Joint Economic Committee*, October 4, 2007. Reproduced by permission of the author.

cant connection between our tremendous use of prison and public safety. As most people know, the U.S. experienced a large crime decline from the early 1990's to the early 2000's and it would seem to make intuitive sense that our significantly increasing prison systems played a major role in that decline.

Increased Prison Use Was Not the Main Cause of Crime Decline

In fact, it is a much more mixed and nuanced story than it would appear. There is some consensus among criminologists and social scientists that over the last decade, our increased use of prison was responsible for some (perhaps around 20–25%) but by no means most of the national crime decline. Additionally, there is also agreement that, going forward, putting even more people in prison will have declining effectiveness as we put more and more people in prison who present less and less of a threat to public safety. At this point, putting greater numbers of people into prison as a way to achieve more public safety is one of the least effective ways we know to decrease crime.

We know, for instance, that even after spending tens of billions of dollars on incarceration, more than half of those leaving prison are back in prison within three years—not a result that anybody should be proud of. We know that targeted spending for effective in-prison and post-prison reentry programs will reduce crime and victims more substantially than prison expansion. We know that diverting people from prison who are not threats to public safety into serious and structured community based alternatives to prison is more effective than simply continuing to incarcerate, at huge expense, these same people. In the same vein, the research shows that increasing high school graduation rates, neighborhood based law enforcement initiatives and increases in employment and wages will also more effectively reduce crime than greater use of prison.

We also know that incarcerating so much of our population and especially the disproportionate incarceration of people of color also comes with other costs as well. Hundreds of thousands of people leave prison annually with no right to vote, no access to public housing, hugely limited abilities to find employment and high levels of drug use and mental illness. These unintended consequences of incarceration ripple through families and communities as those returning home are overwhelmed by seemingly intractable obstacles. Not surprisingly, many people wind up returning to prison in astounding numbers, further draining scarce resources that could be made available to deal with some of these obstacles themselves.

Putting greater numbers of people into prison as a way to achieve more public safety is one of the least effective ways we know to decrease crime.

As someone who used to run the largest city jail system in the country, I know that most people who leave jail and prison do not want to come back. It is a miserable and degrading experience and my colleagues who run these systems and I always marvel about the numbers of people who are leaving prison who want to make good and do good. Once they leave however, they are confronted by such overwhelming barriers on which we currently spend almost no money or attention that no one should be surprised that these same people are back in prison so soon.

We know that states can continue to decrease crime and simultaneously decrease prison populations. New York State, for example, has for the last seven years seen the largest decrease in its prison population of any state in the nation—a decline of 14 percent. The rest of the states increased their prison populations by an average of 12 percent over the same time period. At the same time, violent crime decreased in New

York State by 20 percent compared to just over 1 percent for the rest of the country. Prison populations can drop along with crime and victimization.

Resources Now Used for Prisons Should Be Transferred to More Effective Ways of Increasing Public Safety

If we were serious about using our limited resources most effectively in reducing crime and victimization and increasing public safety, then we would begin to responsibly and systematically transfer some of the resources now used to imprison people to community based prevention, reentry and capacity building. It is important to stress here that this is an issue of public safety. Even putting aside all arguments about efficiency and effectiveness, talking only in terms of public safety, we will all be safer if we begin to reinvest some of the money that now goes to incarcerate people who do not pose a threat to public safety (and who become more of a threat to public safety after they are imprisoned) into other programmatic initiatives both inside and outside the criminal justice system.

We know that states can continue to decrease crime and simultaneously decrease prison populations.

The fact is that almost all the extant research points out that our prison system is too big, too expensive, drains funds away from other essential areas that can more effectively increase public safety, and is harmful to our poorest communities. Despite all this research, however, we continue to imprison more and more people. There is a host of reasons for this ongoing trend including: the attraction of prisons as engines of economic development for rural communities; the financial incentives for public employee unions as well as for the private prison industry in more spending on prisons; the "realities" of the budget process and constrained budgets that limit opportunities to make substantial investments in new initiatives; and the omnipresent hyper-politics that surround issues of crime and punishment in the United States.

These are all formidable obstacles but none should be sufficient to keep us from educating policy makers and the public that there is a better way to be safe and have less crime.

A High Risk of Punishment Reduces Crime

George Will

George Will is a Pulitzer prize winning syndicated columnist as well as a political commentator on ABC television.

Listening to political talk requires a third ear that hears what is not said. Today's near silence about crime probably is evidence of social improvement. For many reasons, including better policing and more incarceration, Americans feel, and are, safer. The *New York Times* has not recently repeated such amusing headlines as "Crime Keeps on Falling, But Prisons Keep on Filling" (1997), "Prison Population Growing Although Crime Rate Drops" (1998), "Number in Prison Grows Despite Crime Reduction" (2000) and "More Inmates, Despite Slight Drop in Crime" (2003).

If crime revives as an issue, it will be through liberal complaints about something that has reduced the salience of the issue—the incarceration rate. And any revival will be awkward for Barack Obama. Liberalism likes victimization narratives and the related assumption that individuals are blank slates on which "society" writes. Hence liberals locate the cause of crime in flawed social conditions that liberalism supposedly can fix.

Last July, Obama said that "more young black men languish in prison than attend colleges and universities." Actually, there are more than twice as many black men ages 18 to 24 in college as there are in jail. Last September he said, "We have a system that locks away too many young, first-time, nonviolent offenders for the better part of their lives." But Heather Mac Donald of the Manhattan Institute, writing in the institute's

George Will, "More Prisoners, Less Crime," *Washington Post*, June 22, 2008, p. B7. Copyright © 2008 Washington Post. Reproduced by permission.

City Journal, notes that from 1999 to 2004, violent offenders accounted for all of the increase in the prison population. Furthermore, Mac Donald cites data indicating that:

> "In the overwhelming majority of cases, prison remains a lifetime achievement award for persistence in criminal offending. Absent recidivism or a violent crime, the criminal-justice system will do everything it can to keep you out of the state or federal slammer."

Obama sees racism in the incarceration rate: "We have certain sentences that are based less on the kind of crime you commit than on what you look like and where you come from." Indeed, in 2006, blacks, who are less than 13 percent of the population, were 37.5 percent of all state and federal prisoners. About one in 33 black men was in prison, compared with one in 79 Hispanic men and one in 205 white men.

From 1999 to 2004, violent offenders accounted for all of the increase in the prison population.

But Mac Donald cites studies of charging and sentencing that demonstrate that the reason more blacks are disproportionately in prison, and for longer terms, is not racism but racial differences in patterns of criminal offenses: "In 2005 the black homicide rate was over seven times higher than that of whites and Hispanics combined. . . . From 1976 to 2005, blacks committed over 52 percent of all murders." Do police excessively arrest blacks? "The race of criminals reported by crime victims matches arrest data."

As for the charge that the incarceration rate of blacks is substantially explained by more severe federal sentences for crack as opposed to powder-cocaine defendants (only 13 states distinguish between the two substances, and these states have small sentence differentials), Mac Donald says:

> "It's going to take a lot more than 5,000 or so [federal] crack defendants a year to account for the 562,000 black

prisoners in state and federal facilities at the end of 2006—or the 858,000 black prisoners in custody overall, if one includes the population of county and city jails."

James Q. Wilson, America's premier social scientist, notes that "the typical criminal commits from 12 to 16 crimes a year (not counting drug offenses)" and says that 10 years of scholarly studies "have shown that states that sent a higher fraction of convicts to prison had lower rates of crime, even after controlling for all of the other ways—poverty, urbanization, and the proportion of young men in the population— that the states differed. A high risk of punishment reduces crime. Deterrence works." It works especially on behalf of blacks, who are disproportionately the victims of crimes by black men.

A recent report by the Pew Center on the States asserts that America incarcerates too many people and in the process diverts money from higher education. Wilson notes that the report does not examine whether the slower growth of public spending on higher education than on prisons may be explained by the surge in private support for public universities. And, Wilson dryly adds, the report does not explore "whether society gets as much from universities as it does from prisons." A good question, but not one apt to be studied in academia.

Long Sentences for Repeat Offenders Lower the Crime Rate

Debra J. Saunders

Debra J. Saunders is a conservative columnist for the San Francisco Chronicle *whose column is carried by newspapers throughout the country.*

In 1994, Californians saw a state criminal justice system that too often let the worst criminals out of prison to wreak destruction and hurt the innocent, only to be sent back to prison for worse crimes.

Fresno parent Mike Reynolds had been pushing Sacramento to pass a "three strikes" measure after the murder of his 18-year-old daughter, Kimber, during a robbery in 1992. Then the rape and murder of Petaluma's 12-year-old Polly Klaas—kidnapped from her home by another violent career criminal—confirmed the voters' worst fears.

The public was ready. The Legislature was afraid. And both Sacramento and California voters passed tough "three strikes" measures.

This being California, there was a pro-criminal lobby that warned against the law, which mandated a 25-year-to-life term for the third offense by criminals who had already committed two serious or violent felonies. It also increased penalties for a second strike.

Longer sentences for career offenders? Horrors.

Critics duly seized on state Department of Corrections forecasts, which ominously predicted that within five years, the prison population would more than double, from 124,813

Debra J. Saunders, "Escaping the Myth of 'Three Strikes' State Prison Law," *San Francisco Chronicle*, July 6, 2008. Copyright © 2008 Creators Syndicate, Inc. By permission of Debra J. Saunders and Creators Syndicate, Inc.

to 245,554. The state would have to build 20 new prisons just to keep up. Within three years, opponents charged, prison spending would outstrip state spending on higher education.

Forecasts Were Wrong

Almost 15 years later, it turns out many of the so-called experts were wrong—and the voters were right. In approving the tough-on-crime measure, California residents didn't have to pay for an inmate population explosion or a bunch of new prisons. What voters got instead was a law that, for the most part, has worked the way it was supposed to.

Fact: California's inmate count was 171,444 last year—far below the grim projections. In part because other prisons already were in the works by the time voters approved "three strikes," Sacramento authorized and completed not 20 new prisons in five years, but only one new prison in the past 14 years. And that happened while the state population grew from 33 million to 38 million.

In approving the tough-on-crime measure, California residents didn't have to pay for an inmate population explosion or a bunch of new prisons.

Yet critics won't even admit they were wrong. What's worse, they want the public to believe that their horror stories actually came to pass.

Every few years, lacking solid statistics, they throw out anecdotes—like the repeat offender who was sentenced under "three strikes" after snatching a pizza from a group of children—to argue that a draconian law has turned California into the Prison State, where petty criminals routinely are put away for life.

Why? Because they don't believe in harsh sentences for career criminals. They want repeat offenders to do long time on the installment plan.

State Sen. George Runner, Republican-Lancaster (Los Angeles County), decided to fight back—with facts. His office put together a seven-page paper—"Who Is In Our State Prisons?"—that debunks many of the oft-repeated "three strikes" misinformation that paints California as a state that over-incarcerates. The paper points to a study released in February [2008] by the Pew Center's Public Safety Performance Project, which placed California in the middle quintile of American states in terms of inmates per capita. For the record, the Pew Center has been critical of "three strikes" laws.

Most Inmates Are Violent or Repeat Offenders

Think that California prisons are teeming with petty offenders? Think again. The Runner paper cites a federal survey that found that 47 percent of California inmates are repeat violent offenders, and 33 percent are repeat nonviolent offenders. Most of the rest are first-time felons who committed crimes against people—think murder, manslaughter, robbery, assault, kidnapping, rape or other sex offenses.

California's crime rate fell dramatically after "three strikes" passed. In 1993, the year before voters approved the measure, the FBI ranked California fourth among the states for total crimes per 100,000 people; in 1999, the murder rate had been cut in half, and California's crime rate had fallen to 29th place.

As far as Runner is concerned, long penalties have made California safer. The "three strikes" law, he said, "keeps people in prison longer. It also makes people's behavior change."

His aide Charlie Fennessey points to burglary convictions as proof that criminals have changed their behavior to keep up with the changed laws. After 1994, he found, some crimes—second-degree burglary and car theft, which are not "three strikes" offenses—increased to earlier levels, but first-degree burglary, a "three strikes crime," remained flat.

's no rational explanation as to why the trends in would be bifurcated," Fennessey said, "unless it had to do with the penalties."

Adam Gelb of the Pew Center provided an alternate explanation. Although he has not studied California's "three strikes" law, he noted, "There is a very common occurrence in courtrooms across the country. It's called 'losing the gun.'" The theory is that criminals are behaving as before, but officers of the court are charging criminals for lesser offenses to avoid "third strike" overkill.

California's crime rate fell dramatically after "three strikes" passed.

"There's no evidence that anyone on the street knows the going rates for what their sentence is going to be or how those punishment rates have increased or decreased over time," Gelb said.

"To say that 'three strikes' has worked, the question is: Compared to what? Since there is so little evidence in any context that longer punishment acts as a general or a special deterrent, it's hard to say that California taxpayers have gotten their money's worth and could not have prevented more crime with a variety of strategies."

The "Three Strikes" Law Locks up Career Criminals

Michael Rushford of the Criminal Justice Legal Foundation in Sacramento conceded that some prosecutors may be undercharging to avoid the longer sentences for repeat offenders. But many prosecutors are not. And the Runner report shows that the "three strikes" law has locked up career criminals—which means that voters got from "three strikes" what they wanted.

Seth Unger of the California Department of Corrections and Rehabilitation told me that more than 1,000 third-strikers entered California prisons in 1995–96, but only 294 third-strikers entered the system 10 years later. Something has changed. Said Unger, "What 'three strikes' was designed to do was cut down on the churning of the prison population. We know that people (who are third-strikers) are not going to be coming back any time soon through the front gates, because they're not getting released."

When "three strikes" was put on the ballot in 1994, I voted no, because I believed that the third strike should apply only to a serious or violent offense. I, too, believed that low-level offenders, not career criminals, would be locked behind bars for decades for petty crimes. So why can't other critics just admit they made a mistake?

"The fundamental reason that critics of tough criminal penalties cannot come to grips with the facts is their unshakable belief that longer sentences inevitably increase prison population," the Runner report said. As if on cue, a February [2008] Pew Center paper asserted that laws like "three strikes" drive up the prison population.

"Opponents of tough criminal laws cannot accept that penalties deter crime," the Runner report said.

California prisons are protecting the public by keeping violent, serious and repeat offenders behind bars.

It's that simple.

It appears that petty criminals have either left the state or changed their ways. If they committed crimes, some at least committed different crimes. And when some small-time thug did get nicked for a small crime, it turned out the guy had a host of priors and couldn't stay out of prison to save his life.

Rather than celebrate the fact that California prisons are protecting the public by keeping violent, serious and repeat offenders behind bars, some California policy leaders actually want to neuter the "three strikes" measure or even get rid of the law.

Perhaps the "three strikes" supporters should follow the example of their opponents: Argue that if we get rid of "three strikes," not only will crime surely go up, but worse, we'll also have to build 20 new prisons. We'll start to spend more on prisons than we spend on higher education. If we get rid of "three strikes," the prison population will explode.

And this time, the dire predictions might turn out to be true.

The Cost of Leaving Criminals Loose Exceeds the Cost of Prisons

Thomas Sowell

Thomas Sowell, a well-known economist and syndicated columnist, is a senior fellow at the Hoover Institution within Stanford University. He is the author of many books.

For more than two centuries, the political left has been preoccupied with the fate of criminals, often while ignoring or downplaying the fate of the victims of those criminals.

So it is hardly surprising that a recent *New York Times* editorial has returned to a familiar theme among those on the left, on both sides of the Atlantic, with its lament that "incarceration rates have continued to rise while crime rates have fallen."

Back in 1997, *New York Times* writer Fox Butterfield expressed the same lament under the headline, "Crime Keeps on Falling, But Prisons Keep on Filling." Then, as now, liberals seemed to find it puzzling that crime rates go down when more criminals are put behind bars.

Nor is it surprising that the left uses an old and irrelevant comparison—between the cost of keeping a criminal behind bars versus the cost of higher education. According to the *Times*, "Vermont, Connecticut, Delaware, Michigan, and Oregon devote as much or more to corrections as they do to higher education."

The relevant comparison would be between the cost of keeping a criminal behind bars and the cost of letting him loose in society. But neither the *New York Times* nor others on the left show any interest in that comparison.

Thomas Sowell, "The Costs of Crime," *Jewish World Review*, March 11, 2008. Copyright © 2008 Creators Syndicate, Inc. By permission of Thomas Sowell and Creators Syndicate, Inc.

In Britain, the total cost of the prison system per year was found to be £1.9 billion, while the financial cost alone of the crimes committed per year by criminals was estimated at £60 billion.

The cost of locking up criminals has to be paid out of government budgets that politicians would prefer to spend on giveaway programs that are more likely to get them re-elected.

The big difference between the two kinds of costs is not just in their amounts. The cost of locking up criminals has to be paid out of government budgets that politicians would prefer to spend on giveaway programs that are more likely to get them re-elected. But the far higher costs of letting criminals loose is paid by the general public in both money and in being subjected to violence.

The net result is that both politicians and ideologues of the left are forever pushing "alternatives to incarceration." These include programs with lovely names like "community supervision" and high-tech stuff like electronic devices to keep track of released criminals' locations.

Just how do you "supervise" a criminal who is turned loose in the community? Assigning someone to be with him, one on one and 24/7, would probably be a lot more expensive than locking him up.

But of course no one is proposing any such thing. Having the released criminal reporting to some official from time to time may be enough to allow the soothing word "supervision" to be used. But it hardly restricts what a criminal does with the other nine-tenths of his time when he is not reporting.

Electronic devices work only when they are being used. Even when they are being used 24/7, they tell you only where the criminal is, not what he is doing. Those released criminals who don't even want that much restriction can of course remove the device and become an escapee, with far less trouble or risk than is required to escape from prison.

Controlling the Statistics

One of the most insidious aspects of "alternatives to incarceration" programs is that those who control such programs often control also the statistical and other information that would be needed to assess the actual consequences of these programs.

They not only control what information is released but to whom it will be released. When officials whose careers are on the line can choose between researchers who view incarceration as being "mean-spirited" toward criminals and other researchers who are much less sympathetic to criminals, who do you think is going to get access to the data?

A study of the treatment of criminals in Britain—"A Land Fit for Criminals" by David Fraser—has several chapters on the games that are played with statistics, in order to make "alternatives to incarceration" programs look successful, even when they are failing abysmally, with tragic results for the public.

Britain has gone much further down the road that the *New York Times* is urging us to follow. In the process, Britain has gone from being one of the most law-abiding nations on earth to overtaking the United States in most categories of crime.

CHAPTER 2

Are Inmates' Constitutional Rights Disregarded in American Prisons?

Chapter Preface

Critics of American prisons argue that the constitutional rights of inmates often are violated. Although prisoners lose most of the freedoms possessed by other citizens, they do have certain rights, such as the right to be held under conditions sufficient to maintain health and the right to practice their own religion. They even have a right other citizens lack: the right to free medical care. Furthermore, the Eighth Amendment to the U.S. Constitution prohibits "cruel and unusual" punishments. This last provision is often the basis of lawsuits filed by inmates and inmate advocates who believe they have been mistreated.

The definition of mistreatment differs not only among people, but across the passage of time. For example, at the time the Bill of Rights was adopted, corporal punishment was not unusual in prisons and was not considered unduly cruel. Even as recently as 1968 a federal circuit court, in overturning an Alabama law that authorized whipping inmates with a five-foot leather strap, thought it necessary to explain that whipping was still allowed in "only two" states and that it "is punishment which, in this last third of the 20th century, runs afoul of the Eighth Amendment . . . [and] offends contemporary concepts of decency and human dignity and precepts of civilization which we profess to possess." Today, the use of corporal punishment as an approved method of maintaining prison discipline would be unthinkable. Prisoners sue if they merely find prison accommodations uncomfortable.

According to U.S. Department of Justice statistics, nearly 40,000 inmate lawsuits were filed in 1995 against prison officials for alleged civil rights violations, most of which were dismissed by judges and court officials as frivolous. (For example, an Arizona death-row prisoner sued corrections officials for taking away his Gameboy electronic game, and an

Arkansas inmate complained that as a result of cruel and unusual punishment he was forced to miss the NFL playoffs.) Among the many suits that have been heard by courts were those of an inmate who was denied access to certain magazines and catalogs; of several who complained that the food they were served was lukewarm rather than hot; and of many who claimed that a prison's failure to evacuate them soon enough during a hurricane caused them to suffer from psychological trauma.

But real abuse does occur in some prisons, and too often officials—as well as most citizens—close their eyes to it. This chapter describes some of the worst situations. In an effort to eliminate frivolous suits, Congress passed a law in 1996 stating that prisoners cannot sue in federal court unless they have suffered physical injury and have exhausted the administrative grievance procedures offered by the prison. This law has had unintended consequences, for abuse can be harmful even when no physical injury is involved and administrative resolution of misconduct by prison officials may be impossible to obtain. Moreover, the majority of abused prisoners do not sue, either because they are poor and uneducated and have no outside supporters, or because they fear retaliation.

In addition to mistreatment caused intentionally or through indifference, many inmates suffer from rights violations simply because of overcrowding and insufficient operating funds in prisons. Class action suits in such cases are proliferating, and in some cases courts are ordering remedies that may include release of prisoners. In others, prison administrators are making sincere and often successful efforts to overcome the problems.

Not all discomfort in prison, however, is unconstitutional. After all, inmates are there because they have committed crimes, and jails and prisons are not intended to be luxurious.

The Reproductive Rights of Women in Prison Are Routinely Ignored

Rachel Roth

Rachel Roth is a feminist scholar focusing on women's reproductive rights. She has worked as a professor and as a research fellow, and she is the author of several books.

An African American woman serving time in a California prison was diagnosed with an ovarian tumor. When she went in for surgery, she was given a hysterectomy to which she had not consented. As she explains:

"[The doctor] tried to convince me to have a hysterectomy, saying that the tumor could grow back, and I was 40 years old and wouldn't have any children anyway. . . . They destroyed all possibilities of me having children. . . . Whether I would or not, I should have been allowed the choice."

As this woman learned the hard way, being in prison often means being denied the right to make choices—even choices about life-altering matters like major surgery or continuing a pregnancy. Because women of color increasingly find their lives affected by prisons, what happens inside prison is a critical issue for the reproductive justice agenda.

This article illustrates some of the ways that imprisonment undermines the health and rights of women who are pregnant and women who are mothers. . . . Courts in the United States have consistently held that people don't automatically lose all their rights when they go to prison; however, there's a difference between having rights in theory and being able to exercise them in real life.

Rachel Roth, "Prisons as Sites of Reproductive Injustice," *Off Our Backs: The Feminist News Journal*, vol. 36, April 1, 2006, pp. 69–71. Copyright © 2006 off our backs, inc. Reproduced by permission.

Prisons reflect and reinforce social disadvantage, confining primarily poor women and men. Women who wind up in prison have usually suffered high rates of physical and sexual abuse and struggled with drug or alcohol addiction. More than 200,000 women are in jail, prison or immigration detention, an eightfold increase since 1980. When probation and parole are included, over one million women are under the authority of the criminal justice system, but white women are the majority of those on probation and women of color are the majority of those behind bars. As of January 2006, for example, more than 82 percent of women serving time in New York state prisons for drug offenses were women of color. These statistics might create the impression that white women don't use drugs, but we know that is not true. What they really show is different rates of surveillance, arrest, prosecution and conviction, as well as unequal access to drug treatment and other resources that might keep women with addiction problems out of the criminal justice system. Many legal and health experts argue that the trend toward strict mandatory sentences has created a system that locks up people who pose little threat to public safety, taking the greatest toll on those who have the fewest advantages to begin with.

Being in prison often means being denied the right to make choices—even choices about life-altering matters like major surgery or continuing a pregnancy.

Being Pregnant on the Inside

Although conservatives sometimes compare prisons to "country clubs," women usually tell a different story. A recent study of pregnant women in the King County Jail in Seattle, Washington, for instance, found that the women "all complained of being uncomfortable, lacking pillows and chairs, having to sit on cold cement, being exposed to toxic cleaning materials, and feeling constantly hungry."

Here's a description of the experience of a South Carolina woman who tested positive for drugs when she was on probation and was sent to jail for the entire seventh month of her pregnancy:

> I was placed in a small one room cell with ten and some-times as many as fifteen other women. I was forced to sleep on a mat on the floor, sometimes near the overflowing toilet. Never being allowed out of the cell, I could do nothing more than stand, squat or lay for the entire thirty days. I was not allowed milk or juice because the other inmates could not have the same. It being the month of August, temperatures were soaring. There was no air conditioning or even a fan. I was truly miserable. I repeatedly requested medical attention, but to no avail. . . . They would promise that I would see the jail doctor the next day, but tomorrow never came.

Surely, these conditions undermine the argument that jailing pregnant women who use drugs is good public policy. The jail environment was unhealthful and no one offered any drug treatment. In addition to addiction, women in prison experience high rates of chronic illnesses such as asthma, diabetes, high blood pressure, Hepatitis C, and HIV, all of which require consistent medical attention and make pregnancy more complicated.

Jails and prisons do not always allow women alternatives to carrying their pregnancies to term.

Women who remain locked up for the duration of their pregnancy have additional concerns: whether they will have to labor and give birth in shackles and whether they will have a safe birth. As part of its investigation of a private prison medical company, *The New York Times* reported on a woman who delivered a premature infant in her cell. The baby was alive but died two days later. The investigation raised serious questions about whether prompt medical attention might have saved the baby's life, or at least spared the mother some suffering.

Cellblock births, miscarriages and newborn deaths are standard stuff in prison exposés. Many who work with women inside suspect that the rates of miscarriage and stillbirth are higher than average. But government agencies don't routinely collect or publish statistics on pregnancy outcomes among women in prison.

Despite their problematic provision of prenatal care, jails and prisons do not always allow women alternatives to carrying their pregnancies to term. Jails and prisons rarely pay for abortion care. It is common practice to require a woman to pay for an abortion, and often to pay the cost of transportation and staff time for the officers who transport her as well. Some jails have set up additional hurdles, such as requiring a woman to get a court order authorizing the jail to take her to a clinic. All of these requirements burden women who are poor and delay their access to time-sensitive medical care. When women have turned to the courts for help, the courts always vindicate their right to abortion, and in only one case has the requirement to get a court order been upheld—but sometimes, the ruling comes so late that they decide to continue the pregnancy, or are forced to, because it is no longer possible to get an abortion in the state.

All of these examples highlight the failure of government officials to meet their obligations to women who have been taken into custody, including adequately treating their serious medical needs and safeguarding their fundamental constitutional rights.

Mothering on the Inside . . . and Afterward

About five percent to six percent of women who enter jail or prison are pregnant, but at least 65 percent are already mothers of children under eighteen. Maintaining relationships with those children is incredibly challenging, because of limited visiting hours, the exorbitant cost of collect phone calls, and distance from home. In many states, the one prison for women is in a rural area, even though most of the women come from cities. Moreover, some women are sent to serve their time in other states. The Hawaii prison system, for instance, sends about half of all adults to serve their time in privately run prisons on the mainland; Native Hawaiians are over-represented among those shipped out. Of 120 Hawaiian women—almost all mothers—marking time in a rural Kentucky prison, not a single one has seen her children since arriving in the former mining town.

Women who make it out of prison with their legal relationship to their children intact may still find that they cannot be reunited with them.

Compounding these geographical and logistical difficulties created by prison systems are public policies that jeopardize the parental rights of women whose children go into foster care. The median sentence for women in state prisons is 60 months, but most states have a policy to begin terminating parental rights after a child has been in foster care for 15 months in a 22-month period. The policies do not make exceptions for women in prison, even if they have never been accused of neglecting or abusing their children.

Women who make it out of prison with their legal relationship to their children intact may still find that they cannot be reunited with them. If they have a felony drug conviction, as so many do, in many states they will find that they are no longer eligible for public housing, food stamps or loans to go back to school—resources that would help them to make a new start and build a better future for themselves and their families. Given the racial distribution of poverty and the racial biases of criminal justice administration, these policies fall especially heavily on women of color, permanently undermining their right to be mothers.

Finally, women of color are also dramatically affected by the incarceration of men—including men who are the fathers of their children. Racial patterns of incarceration are similar for both sexes, but incarceration rates are much higher for men; in 2005, more than half a million African American men ages 20–39 were serving time. These men will face similar obstacles to resuming life in the community when they are released.

The Costs of Punishment

Medical neglect in prisons and the erosion of parental rights both fit into a long history of reproductive oppression suffered by poor women and women of color, including the sale of children under slavery, the forced removal of Native children to government boarding schools, sterilization abuse, bans on public funding for abortion, and punitive welfare policies.

This state of affairs is especially troubling for women who are "caught in the net" of the criminal justice system because of a health problem—drug addiction—and poverty. If the United States provided treatment to all who want it, then many women would never wind up in the criminal justice system in the first place, let alone serving long prison sentences. Individual women and their families would be better served by real community-based alternatives to incarceration—and so would everyone else. U.S. taxpayers currently foot the bill for the biggest prison system in the world, at a cost of $60 billion a year, instead of investing in priorities like schools, child care and health care that could foster a more egalitarian and less punitive culture.

Male Rape in Prison Is Still Not Taken Seriously

Dan Bell

Dan Bell is a journalist who now works in London.

Even as the gates slammed shut and he stepped out into the roar of the main cellblock, T.J. Parsell was still in denial. He had landed in prison after a drunken prank with a toy gun netted him $50 and two and a half years. His older brother, who had served some brief jail time, had given him some advice: Look tough. Show no fear. Be a man.

But even if Parsell could have kept his shoulders back, his chin cocked and the panic out of his eyes as he walked beneath five stories of barred cells, through the echoes of slamming doors, the clatter of chow trays and the shouts of 500 inmates, they already knew: This paper-thin kid with a desperate game face was fresh meat. Barely six weeks later, according to Parsell, he had been drugged, gang-raped by three inmates and "sold" to a fourth with the flip of a coin. He was 17 years old.

Parsell's story is horrifying, but hardly surprising. And therein lies a paradox: If prison rape is as prevalent as it is thought to be, it stands as one of the most appallingly frequent human rights abuses in America. But as a matter of public concern, when the victims are male, the issue remains little more than a dirty joke.

In 2001 Human Rights Watch [HRW] attempted to turn off the canned laughter. Drawing on testimonies from 200 prisoners in thirty-four states, HRW released a report titled "No Escape: Male Rape in US Prisons." The findings suggested that male rape, often accompanied by almost unimaginable

Dan Bell, "'They Deserve It,'" *Nation*, vol. 283, July 10, 2008, pp. 18–24. Copyright © 2008 by The Nation Magazine/The Nation Company, Inc. Reproduced by permission.

violence, is widespread throughout the US prison system. The report was damning enough to help convince Congress to pass the optimistically named 2003 Prison Rape Elimination Act [PREA]. In writing PREA, Congress estimated that 13 percent of inmates had been sexually assaulted. Even if that is (as many experts believe) a conservative estimate, it translates into a stunning number of victims. "Nearly 200,000 inmates now incarcerated have been or will be the victims of prison rape," the act states. "The total number of inmates who have been sexually assaulted in the past 20 years likely exceeds 1,000,000."

The act is intended to tackle rape in both male and female prisons; there is no reliable gender breakdown of prison rape victims, but 93 percent of America's prison population is male.

Despite the bold promise implied by its name. PREA hasn't made a dent in the statistics so far. Although the act sets out to define new standards for detection, prevention, reduction and punishment of prison rape, no new standards have yet been established—and when they are, they are unlikely to go into effect before 2010. Even then, it is by no means certain that they will be effectively enforced.

But the problem goes deeper than inadequate legislation. The prevailing social attitude toward male prison rape was typified by California Attorney General Bill Lockyer back in 2001, when Enron CEO Ken Lay was in the news. "I would love to personally escort Lay," Lockyer said, "to an 8-by-10 cell that he could share with a tattooed dude who says, Hi, my name is Spike, honey."

Male rape, often accompanied by almost unimaginable violence, is widespread throughout the US prison system.

"I think in a lot of ways this issue is where the women's issue was about thirty years ago," says Lara Stemple, former executive director of Stop Prisoner Rape, the only national organization dedicated to advocating on behalf of prison-rape survivors. "People still make jokes about men being raped that people would never make about women." If the male victim is behind bars, the problem is compounded. Louise Kindley, a veteran rape-crisis counselor who recently opened New York's first program for male survivors, says, "There is an idea that they deserve it."

A Teenage Victim

As a first-time teenage offender, Parsell fit the profile of a prison rape victim to a T. After an initial six weeks on lock-down, he was transferred into the general population at Riverside Correctional Facility, at that time (the late 1970s) one of Michigan's three "close-custody" security prisons—one security level down from maximum. It could hardly have been a worse place for him to land: In a 2000 investigation of medium- and maximum-security prisons in the state, PREA commissioner Cindy Struckman-Johnson surveyed 1,788 inmates. One in ten said they had been raped, and one in five had experienced "pressured or forced sexual contact."

Parsell didn't know that, of course. But he did know that he was scared and lonely. So despite his brother's warning that any sign of weakness would turn him into a victim, when an older inmate came up and started talking to him on his first day at Riverside, Parsell opened a chink in his exhausted defenses. "The guy was just very friendly," he remembers, "and he said, You know, after count [the roll call of inmates] why don't you come down to chow with me?" By late morning the following day, Parsell and his new friend, Ron, were in the card room with two other inmates, dipping into a plastic bag full of homemade hooch. The old Maxwell House coffee jar Parsell was drinking out of never seemed to get empty.

It took about half an hour for the Thorazine they'd spiked his drink with to hit. Suddenly Parsell couldn't think straight. He couldn't understand what was being said to him, and he couldn't understand why he couldn't understand. It was, he says, like watching a film with pieces of blank tape spliced into it: "skips, like mini-blackouts," flashes followed by darkness.

Then he was back in one of the dormitories. Four inmates were waiting for him. It was only then that Parsell began to understand what was happening. But by the time the panic hit, it was too late. Ron shoved Parsell onto one of the bunks and another two inmates tore off his pants. Even if Parsell hadn't been half their size, with the Thorazine he didn't have a chance. . . .

Both survivors and advocates are certain that a large portion of sexual assaults in prisons could be avoided if young, vulnerable inmates were not housed with violent predators.

By that afternoon he had been raped by another two inmates and traded into sexual slavery with a coin toss. His new owner wasn't one of his rapists, but another inmate named Slo-Drag. The rest of the prison knew by the following day. "That's Slo-Drag's boy," they said as they brushed past. Ron thought it was hilarious; he could hardly stop laughing.

Prison Rape Could Be Prevented

Parsell, now president of Stop Prisoner Rape's board of directors, speaks widely about his experiences. He believes that his rape, like many others, could have been prevented. Both survivors and advocates are certain that a large portion of sexual assaults in prisons could be avoided if young, vulnerable inmates were not housed with violent predators, and if corrections officials made it clear to new inmates that they will quickly and conscientiously respond when violence occurs. "There has to be a climate where inmates can report effectively, yet be protected from retaliation," says Struckman-Johnson.

But the fact is, many prison guards couldn't care less. In a study of Midwestern prisons in 1991, Helen Eigenberg of the University of Tennessee at Chattanooga found that 16 percent of officers thought inmates deserved rape if they were homosexual; 17 percent if they "dressed or talked in feminine ways"; 23 percent if they had "previously engaged in consensual sexual acts in prison"; and 24 percent if they had taken "money or cigarettes for consensual sexual acts prior to a rape." An earlier study Eigenberg conducted in Texas echoed those findings.

Even prison administrators admit to widespread indifference. A 2004 survey of executive-level staff, commissioned by the National Institute of Corrections, concluded: "Sexual assault has been accepted in the past" and "there has been an expectation that it will occur. In some prison environments practices exist that encourage or facilitate sexual assault." . . .

The fact is, many prison guards couldn't care less.

The PREA legislation promised to make certain that prison rape would no longer be treated with indifference. The act funded a nationwide study of prison rape by the Bureau of Justice Statistics (BJS) and created a PREA commission to assess the data and recommend a set of standards to the Attorney General. Examples of those being considered are protocols for separating vulnerable inmates from predators and hiring independent prison ombudsmen [someone who handles complaints and attempts to resolve conflict in an even-handed way] to hear complaints of abuse. The Justice Department will issue policies, based on the commission's recommendations, that will become law in all federal prisons. States will have to adopt the federal guidelines or lose 5 percent of their federal funding—serious money.

The Prison Rape Elimination Act May Not Be Enforced

Unfortunately, the pace of this "Elimination Act" is glacial. . . . Once the guidelines go into effect, enforcement is likely to be a problem. PREA authorizes no civil or criminal penalties for prison guards or administrators who preside over institutionalized rape. The law does require administrators from the nation's three facilities with the highest incidence of rape to come before a review panel each year to explain themselves. But this public shaming is, so far the only real threat faced by the administrators. And even the review panels and fact-finding by the BJS face an uncertain future. Funding for the research is guaranteed by PREA only until 2010. "There is just no way to anticipate either the funding stream or what data collections will look like that far down the road," says Timothy Hughes, a BJS statistician charged with directing the prison-rape data collection. "If there was no funding stream, and the collections didn't continue, then I would imagine that there would be no review panel, because there would be no data to review."

But if the review process looks toothless, the legislation is weakest of all in its pocketbook. Neither the commission nor the Attorney General is allowed to recommend measures "that would impose substantial additional costs" on prison authorities. "We are restrained by the bill," says Struckman-Johnson. "These have to be practical, inexpensive ideas that we put forth. We can't say, Build new prisons."

There is some funding available for states to establish "zero tolerance" programs. Through the Bureau of Justice Assistance (BJA), Congress authorized $40 million a year through 2010 when it passed PREA. But those appropriations still have to make their way into the federal budget every year, and the money has been disappearing fast. In 2004 $37.2 million was appropriated for zero tolerance. But by 2006 the figure had dropped to less than half that. Although not yet finalized, the

2007 budget request has shrunk even further, to a paltry $2 million. It appears that zero tolerance is on its way to zero funding.

Unfortunately, the pace of [the Prison Rape] Elimination Act is glacial.... Once the guidelines go into effect, enforcement is likely to be a problem.

New York State was one of sixteen states to receive zero-tolerance funding in 2004 for its Department of Corrections. Its $1 million federal grant was matched by another $1 million from state and local sources. Some of this money was supposed to help pay for risk assessment, screening and separating vulnerable inmates from potential predators. But in the end, the vast majority of the $2 million has been earmarked for surveillance cameras in the Albion Correctional Facility for Women, and in New York City Department of Corrections facilities.

PREA also authorized a small amount, $5 million a year, to educate and train corrections officers across the country. By fiscal years 2005 and 2006, as the momentum for prison-rape reform continued to fizzle, the annual appropriation for training had dipped to just $1 million each year—a true drop in the bucket.

In one state, at least, there are encouraging signs that reform is possible. After California legislators heard testimony from Parsell and others, the State Assembly passed a law requiring the Department of Corrections to provide inmates with handbooks on sexual assault; adopt practices that will separate vulnerable prisoners from sexual predators; collect accurate data and make it publicly available; and bring rape-crisis services into prisons. The legislation also created a state office to "ensure confidential reporting and impartial resolution of sexual abuse complaints." Other states have begun to take steps, says Katherine Hall-Martinez, co-executive director of Stop Prison Rape, "but no state has been as quick and aggressive as California." Still, even the California law doesn't include penalties for prison administrators.

In 2002, twenty-four years after he was raped at Riverside, T.J. Parsell walked into a Midtown Manhattan video store and, found the sales assistants laughing at an episode of the TV series *Oz*, in which an inmate is raped. "The guys could have taken out a little knife and just poked me in the gut," Parsell says. The experience led him to become an activist, and ultimately to write a book about his experiences.

Female Prison Inmates Are Sexually Assaulted by Guards

Jeff Seidel

Jeff Seidel is a staff writer for the Detroit Free Press.

Toni Bunton heard the guard coming down the hallway. He wore cheap cologne, and his breath smelled like cigarettes. He scuffed his boots against the floor and opened the door to her cell in Scott Correctional Facility, a women's prison in Plymouth Township.

"Come here," he ordered.

The guard pulled Bunton into a bathroom. She wore jogging pants, a T-shirt and socks. She was the guard's prized possession, a pretty young thing, as he said, "just the way I like 'em,"—short and cute with brown hair, brown eyes and porcelain skin.

"Shhh!" he demanded. He yanked down her underwear and pushed her against the sink.

"No!" she screamed in her head. "No, please, no!" But she was scared to death, and the words wouldn't come out. "I'm choking, please, stop, I'm going to die," she thought.

And he raped her.

No one, no one in this country, no one in a civilized society is sentenced to be raped and assaulted in prison.

Bunton said nothing. It would become the theme of her life, a way to survive the next 16 years in prison.

When he was done, he stepped back. "Shhh!" he said, with his finger to his lips. He smiled and left. Bunton stood there, numb, her pants at her ankles.

Jeff Seidel, "Sexual Assaults on Female Inmates Went Unheeded," *Detroit Free Press*, January 4, 2009. Copyright © 2009 Detroit Free Press Inc. Reproduced by permission of the Detroit Free Press.

Bunton said she was raped seven more times by prison guards between 1993 and 1996. She is among more than 500 women who say they were sexually assaulted by guards at several Michigan prisons in the 1990s as officials ignored or dismissed warnings by human rights groups that male guards were preying on female inmates.

A class-action lawsuit against the Michigan Department of Corrections has already yielded verdicts reaching an estimated $50 million, when interest and fees are included. And that's only for the first 18 women. With most yet to testify, and lawyers for the state insisting they have no intention of settling, Michigan's beleaguered taxpayers could face hundreds of millions of dollars in damages.

"A prison is not supposed to turn you back out to society with more harm than when you came in," said Deborah La-Belle, an Ann Arbor civil rights lawyer who led a team that sued on behalf of the women. "No one, no one in this country, no one in a civilized society is sentenced to be raped and assaulted in prison."

The State's Defense: Why Didn't They Speak Up?

It wasn't just the rapes. Many women said they were routinely molested by guards who took advantage of rules that required them to meet a daily quota of pat-down searches for weapons, drugs or other contraband. Inmates said guards ran their hands over the women's legs, buttocks and breasts under the guise of security. When it became clear the guards wouldn't be punished, some grew so brazen that they fondled women in front of other inmates and guards, or openly masturbated in the prison yard, according to trial testimony.

It is against the law for guards to have sexual contact with prisoners, even if there is consent. Some guards convinced women to submit to ongoing sexual relations in return for "protecting" them from fellow guards.

For years, Bunton kept quiet. She was afraid to speak up. She was a prisoner, after all, a convicted felon, afraid the allegations would not be taken seriously. Afraid of retaliation. But after years of delay, the case involving the first 10 women, including Bunton, reached a courtroom last winter [2008].

The state had a simple defense: These women are prisoners, and prisoners lie; if something did happen, it was the act of a few rogue guards; and if something did happen, the women didn't report it. So how could the Department of Corrections prevent what it didn't know was happening? The state said it thoroughly investigated any allegations it knew about and the claims of abuse were exaggerated.

Some guards convinced women to submit to ongoing sexual relations in return for "protecting" them from fellow guards.

"To say the department just sat back and did nothing, just let everybody run the place is just totally false," Allan Soros, an assistant attorney general, said at the first trial. Nonetheless, a series of human rights reports throughout the 1990s said sexual assaults on female inmates were rampant and corrections officials tolerated the climate.

Since then, the state says it has made changes. They include refined work rules to prevent sexual misconduct or harassment by guards, tougher legal penalties for guards who have sexual contact with inmates and a policy to refer allegations to the Michigan State Police, as well Corrections Department internal affairs, for investigation.

LaBelle said the legal action, at its heart, was about human rights. About women coming out of the shadows and getting a chance to tell their stories.

Bunton and the other women who testified are no saints. The group includes convicted murderers, thieves and drug dealers. But Bunton, now 35, says it's important to listen to all of them, no matter their past.

"People don't know what goes on inside prison," Bunton said. "I think a lot of people don't care, unless it directly affects them. I want people to know this is going on in your backyard, and you might not care because it might not affect you, but you should care. This is not really about sexual harassment. This is about civil rights, basic fundamental rights of human beings."

A Favor Turns to Murder

Bunton knew the guys as Pook and Timbo and Poodle, friends of her cousin, all of them teens in Detroit. They were planning to sell marijuana, and the deal was set, but they needed a ride, according to Bunton. One of the guys said: "Let's steal a car."

Bunton said: "Oh, no, I'll take you." At the time, she said, it didn't sound monumental or deadly, a trip that would ruin the lives of nearly all involved.

"I know it's stupid now," Bunton said recently. "I think it is really stupid . . . but at 17, uh, I didn't see the harm in it."

Bunton had a clean record, no history of drug involvement. According to records from the case, she dropped off the teens at a gas station on Livernois in southwest Detroit. "Just drive around the block and come back," she said she was told.

This is not really about sexual harassment. This is about civil rights, basic fundamental rights of human beings.

She was in a white Mustang, and was halfway around the block when she heard gunshots. She began driving faster and ended up going down a dead-end street. Bunton turned the car around and, now, the teens were running toward her—Pook and Timbo and Poodle—and they were waving guns. She said later she had no idea they had guns. They jumped into her car, screaming and shouting, saying they had "popped" somebody.

The two buyers had been shot. Police found Omar Kaji, 19, dead from a single gunshot wound to his head. He was slumped at the wheel of a Monte Carlo. He had a 9-mm automatic pistol. His twin, Ayman, was shot several times. He was lying by the passenger door.

Later, police would suggest, it was a setup—by both sides. The buyers didn't have money to make a deal. All they had was a wad of blank paper, wrapped with a $20 bill. The sellers, meanwhile, didn't have any pot.

Ayman Kaji admitted that he and his brother planned to steal the marijuana. He identified one of the teens with Bunton that night, Jose Burgos, 16, as the shooter. "He got in the car and just started shooting," Kaji said. Kaji remains paralyzed from the neck down.

A Murder Conviction and a Harsh Sentence

Bunton said she dropped the teens off and went home.

The next day, police took her to police headquarters for questioning. After signing a statement detailing her role, Bunton thought she was going home. She said she didn't know that, even though she didn't pull the trigger, she could be held just as culpable as the teen who did.

Burgos was convicted of first-degree murder and is serving life in prison. The other two teens never went to trial.

Kaji was wheeled into court at Bunton's sentencing. He spoke in a whisper, and the emotional scene tugged on the heart of Judge Clarice Jobes. Three years later, in a 1994 newspaper interview about her retirement from Detroit Recorder's Court, Jobes singled out the case as an example of the endless violence she saw from the bench and admitted that she was so moved that she later cried.

Bunton was convicted of second-degree murder, armed robbery and assault with intent to murder. She was sentenced to 25 to 50 years, a term that some legal experts now say appeared excessive, given her role. . . .

Bunton has accepted responsibility for the tragedy, even as she insists she was only the getaway driver. "I feel horrible," she says now. "I deserve to be punished, and you know, I have spent half of my life thinking about the (Kaji) family. . . . I am so sorry." . . .

[Scott Correctional Facility] was Bunton's new home, a facility she described as wild, with few rules and almost no physical boundaries between the guards and inmates.

At 4 foot 11, Bunton was small and meek when she entered prison. One day, she was taking a shower, and one of the male guards pulled back the curtain. "I'm naked," Bunton said, scrambling to cover her body.

"Oh, hush," the guard said. "I got a wife at home, I know what it all looks like."

Search Policy Becomes an Excuse for Sexual Contact

At Scott, as in every Michigan prison at the time, every guard was required to pat down five prisoners every shift for weapons, food, drugs, whatever. It didn't matter which prisoners they picked. Some officers did it the proper way, quickly and with professionalism. But others exploited this directive, picking out the pretty women to search, the ones who were young and had long sentences.

Bunton said she was a daily target. "The officers would come and feel us up whenever they wanted," she said. A guard "would cup the breast. He would rub his hands down your stomach and around your thighs and buttocks, legs. All the way up your thighs, to the end."

State prison officials would claim later they had no idea that some guards abused the search policies by sexually assaulting the women. They said they properly trained officers and had written policies against improper behavior. The rules have changed since. Men are not assigned to housing units and are not allowed to pat down women.

But the Michigan Women's Commission reported in 1993 there was an alarming level of sexual abuse and harassment by state prison guards. In 1995, the U.S. Department of Justice found "pervasive" sexual abuse in Michigan women's prisons.

In 1996, Human Rights Watch released a report documenting sexual harassment, sexual abuse and privacy violations by guards and other employees in Michigan prisons. The report, based on interviews with prisoners and prison rights advocates, cited rapes by guards in a "highly sexualized and excessively hostile" environment. "Rather than seeking to end such abuse, the Michigan Department of Corrections has consistently refused to acknowledge that there is a problem of sexual misconduct in its women's prisons." . . .

Other Inmates' Stories Show Pattern of Abuse

Bunton's account echoed the abuse testimony of other women at the civil trial last year in front of Judge Timothy Connors. . . .

Amy Black, who also entered prison at 17, had sex with a guard two or three times a week over several years. "He promised he would treat me right and make sure none of the other officers were bothering me," said Black, serving life for murder. "He promised to make sure I was safe." She ended the relationship when she found out that he was having sex with another prisoner, who she had heard had a sexually transmitted disease.

"For him, I think it was about sex," Black said. "For me, it was about staying alive."

'Make It Your Garden, Where You Can Grow'

Bunton learned to keep her mouth shut. The guards controlled everything: when she ate, when she slept, when she went to the bathroom, when she spoke. Each time she was raped, each time she was groped, Bunton buried the pain deep inside.

Dr. Frank Ochberg, a psychologist who examined Bunton in prison, later told jurors she had been "systemically, overtly degraded" by the assaults, the "humanity just beaten out of her."

"I call them battle scars because they never go away," Bunton said. "Being a prisoner is the lowest you can be in life. Being a female prisoner is so much worse."

She tried to hide in her cell, reading and thinking and praying. She kept her mouth shut.

"There was someone very close to me, who told me a long time ago, 'Scott Correctional Facility is a very bad place,'" Bunton said. "'But it is up to you to find the good in the place. So you can look around in that very bad place and you can make it your garden, where you can grow, no matter what is going on around you. It's up to you to remove yourself from the bad and only concentrate on the good.'

"So that's what I did. I made that place my garden. I grew."

Education Gives Her Courage to Tell Her Story

Bunton, a high school dropout, focused on her education, earning associate's and bachelor's degrees in business administration and a master's degree from a correspondence program.

She earned vocational certificates in food management, computers and graphic arts. She became a yoga teacher and fitness trainer. "Every time I accomplished something, I felt better about myself," she said.

She grew stronger. She gained confidence and found her voice. Toni Bunton, inmate No. 221034, was learning to stand up for herself.

After suffering in silence, she took a gamble. She summoned the courage to join a lawsuit against the Michigan Department of Corrections. She decided to speak up and tell her story, hoping it would force some changes, hoping that it would end the attacks. . . .

After years of sexual brutality Bunton found there were people—strangers, even—willing to fight with her: civil rights lawyers and law students at the University of Michigan.

They would push for her voice to be heard in court. They would fight for her freedom.

Minority Religions Are Not Accommodated by Prison Policies

Bob Ritter

Bob Ritter is an attorney and legal coordinator of the Appignani Humanist Legal Center of the American Humanist Association.

For the first time in history more than one in every 100 American adults is in jail or prison according to a Pew Center report released in late February [2008]. With more than 2.3 million people being housed in our prisons and jails at a cost to taxpayers of $55 billion a year, we should, as always, allow prisoners the freedom to exercise their religious rights. But can we afford to?

To further accommodate the free exercise of religion and to diminish the effect of Supreme Court decisions such as *Turner v. Safley* (whereby the constitutional rights of inmates may be infringed by regulations "reasonably related to legitimate penological interests"), Congress passed the Religious Freedom Restoration Act (RFRA) in 1993 and the Religious Land Use and Institutionalized Persons Act (RLUIPA) in 2000. These federal laws provide that government may only "substantially" burden a person's exercise of religion if it can demonstrate that the restriction is necessary to further a compelling interest (a very high legal standard) and, even then, only if there is no other less restrictive alternative. Of course, what constitutes a substantial burden is determined by the courts and is difficult for the parties of a case to predict.

Civil Rights Commission Testimony

Fast-forward to a briefing of the U.S. Commission on Civil Rights on February 8, 2008. The commission brought together

Bob Ritter, "Special Report: Commission on Civil Rights Examines Prisoners' Free Exercise of Religion," *Humanist*, vol. 68, May/June 2008, pp. 7–9. Copyright © 2008 by the American Humanist Association. Reproduced by permission.

a diverse group of experts to discuss issues arising out of RLUIPA. In particular, the commission focused on the rights of prisoners to practice their religion freely; the rights of faith-based organizations to offer inmate services on equal terms with secular organizations; questions concerning the separation of church and state; and questions of prison security.

We should, as always, allow prisoners the freedom to exercise their religious rights. But can we afford to?

During more than three hours of testimony, the commission heard that religious accommodation in prisons was hampered by a number of factors including security needs, lack of religious materials, limited resources (both money and staff for additional programs), indifference or hostility to minority religions by prison staff, and lack of chaplains of particular faiths. In addition, prison procedures and practices thwarted resolution of complaints by prisoners. There was even testimony that some complaints were thrown in the trash. This is particularly troublesome because a prisoners' access to the courts generally depends upon the exhausting of administrative remedies.

One might assume that the briefing would favor faith-based groups because the political affiliation of commissioners is predominantly Republican (President [George W.] Bush appointed four of the eight members; the other half was appointed by Congress). Refreshingly, the entire panel represented a broad spectrum of interests with no one view dominating the briefing.

The expected fireworks between Patrick Nolan, vice president of Chuck Colson's Prison Fellowship, and Alex Luchenitser, senior litigation counsel at Americans United for Separation of Church and State, never materialized. Americans United brought a lawsuit in 2003 challenging the Iowa Corrections Department's support for Prison Fellowship Ministries' InnerChange Freedom Initiative, a prison program that trains inmates in evangelical Christianity. On June 2, 2006, the U.S. Court of Appeals for the 8th Circuit held that Iowa's funding of the program violated the establishment clause of the First Amendment. No prisoners have been permitted to join the program since last year, and the state decided to discontinue the program at the Newton Correctional Facility in April.

Resistance to Religion in Prison Is Widespread

Instead of speaking at length on Prison Fellowship efforts, Nolan told the commission that "resistance to religion is widespread" because facilitating religious practices in prison is more work for prison staff. He noted that access to religious materials is a problem (reporting that he was denied a Bible while serving a two-year sentence for campaign contribution violations) and that some religious materials mailed to prisoners are thrown away. Nolan further told the commission that limiting religion to one night a week (a common practice) is "arbitrary." Finally, Nolan concluded that single-faith settings (like InnerChange) should be allowed so long as others are allowed their single-faith setting.

> *Administrators and security staff view all faith practices from the perspective of the dominant faith.*

Countering Nolan's testimony, Luchenitser told the commission that "tax dollars should not be used to support prison ministry programs that coerce inmates into participation." Luchenitser said that in those cases where religious groups want to take tax aid to provide faith-based services, they should first agree to run secular programs and drop all forms of religiously based discrimination from their hiring policies.

Perhaps the most interesting testimony was given by Patrick McCollum, a Wiccan priest who provides workshops to chaplains of all faiths and advises various government agencies regarding chaplaincy and religious practices. Focusing his remarks primarily on the accommodation of Wicca in correctional institutions, McCollum stated that discrimination against non-traditional religions was common. The reason for this, he said, is what he calls "the Dominant Religion Lens Factor," whereby administrators and security staff view all faith practices from the perspective of the dominant faith. McCollum shared the following example: He arrived at a prison to conduct a Wiccan service and had the prisoners arrange their chairs in a circle, which is a typical Wiccan practice. Almost immediately, prison personnel stepped in and said they couldn't conduct their services sitting in a circle due to security concerns. Instead, McCollum was forced to conduct his services from a pulpit with the chairs lined up in rows (typical of dominant religions), resulting in the denial of their right to practice their faith in its traditional manner. The story has a happy ending—McCollum was eventually allowed to hold services in a circle. (Did they figure the shape wasn't so dangerous after all?)

In the end, the powers of the commission are limited, but even so the results of the February briefing and other written comments will be compiled in a report sent to the president and Congress later this year [2008]. Given that RFRA and RLUIPA are as pro-free exercise of religion as you can get under our Constitution and more money for prisons is unlikely, I don't anticipate the Commission on Civil Rights recommending any major legislative changes. Instead, I believe the focus of its report will be the need to better train and sensitize prison personnel concerning prisoner's rights to freely exercise their religion or lack thereof. They can at least afford to do that.

Absent Physical Injury, Prison Abuse Victims Cannot Sue in Federal Courts

Stephen B. Bright

Stephen B. Bright is president and senior counsel of the Southern Center for Human Rights. He also teaches at Yale and at Georgetown Law School.

Much of the support for the PLRA [Prison Litigation Reform Act] was based on arguments that demonized prisoners and trivialized their concerns. However, the men, women and children who are incarcerated in this country are not members of a faceless, undifferentiated mass unworthy of protection of the law. They are individuals, who vary considerably in the crimes they have committed, the lives they have led, their potential to be productive members of society, and their commitment to lead useful and productive lives. Most of them will return to society. They have families and friends who care about their safety. A significant number are mentally ill, have limited intellectual functioning, are addicted to substances or have a combination of these features. . . .

People in this country and around the world were horrified by images of Abu Ghraib [a prison in Iraq], as undoubtedly were all the members of this Subcommittee. What few people know is that if such conduct occurs in a prison or jail in this country, those subject to it would have no redress in the federal courts due to the "physical injury" requirement of the PLRA.

We [the Southern Center for Human Rights] had such a case. Officers who hid their identity by not wearing or by cov-

Stephen B. Bright, "Testimony Regarding the Prison Abuse Remedies Act," *United States House of Representatives, Subcommittee on Crime, Terrorism and Homeland Security of the Committee on the Judiciary*, April 22, 2008. Reproduced by permission of the author.

ering their badges rampaged through a prison—swearing at inmates, calling some of them "faggots"; destroying their property; hitting, pushing and kicking them; choking some with batons; and slamming some to the ground. The male inmates were ordered to strip and subjected to full body cavity searches in view of female staff. Some were left standing naked for 20 minutes or more outside their cells, while women staff members pointed and laughed at them. Some were ordered to "tap dance" while naked—to stand on one foot and hold the other in their hands, then switch, and rapidly go from standing on one foot to the other. The Court of Appeals for the Eleventh Circuit held that this conduct did not satisfy the physical injury requirement of the PLRA.

Other courts have found the physical injury requirement was not satisfied by

- a "bare allegation of sexual assault" even where male prisoners alleged that a corrections officer had sexually assaulted them repeatedly over a span of hours,

- prisoners being housed in cells soiled by human waste and subjected to the screams of psychiatric patients,

- a prisoner being forced to stand in a 2½-foot wide cage for 13 hours, naked for the first 10 hours, in acute pain, with clear, visible swelling in leg that had been previously injured in car accident,

- a prisoner who complained of suffering second-degree burns to the face.

Prisoners Who Are Degraded Cannot Bring Suit

There are far more cases that are never brought or [are] promptly dismissed because of the physical injury requirement. Prior to enactment of the PLRA, we brought suit on behalf of women who were constantly splattered with bodily waste as a result of being housed with severely mentally ill women. Our clients could not sleep at night because the mentally ill women shrieked and carried on loud conversations, often with themselves. We would not bring that suit today. Our clients were degraded, they were deprived of sleep, but they suffered no physical injury.

The physical injury requirement [of the PLRA] ... provides incentives for officials to argue that truly reprehensible and degrading conduct was acceptable.

Recently, we have concluded that suits could not be brought by men who complained of being chained to a bed in one case and a grate in the floor in another, each left for several days without breaks and so they had to defecate and urinate on themselves repeatedly, or by women who complained that officers barged into their shower and toilet areas without announcing themselves, opened the shower curtains and made sexual comments to them.

Denying money damages is significant for several reasons. Damages awards create incentives for prison administrators to improve policies and training and [to] not retain officers who abuse prisoners. Beyond that, the physical injury requirement changes the framework of the debate because it provides incentives for officials to argue that truly reprehensible and degrading conduct was acceptable because it did not produce a "physical injury."

The "physical injury" provision of the PLRA should be repealed.

Medical Care for Prison Inmates Has Been Improved

Mark Taylor

Mark Taylor is a reporter for Modern Healthcare.

The multibillion-dollar business of caring for the nation's 2.2 million prisoners and inmates continues to snare headlines, sap government resources and pose enormous financial and delivery challenges for the federal, state and local government agencies charged with providing those services and the taxpayers who fund them.

But in an era of shrinking government budgets for social services, the prison healthcare system—a "mini me" version of the $2 trillion overall U.S. healthcare system—presents a moral dilemma to America's national conscience. How does the country fairly and adequately care for those convicted of crimes or awaiting trial without siphoning too much governmental funding from other vital and more popular services for the general population?

In response to prisoner complaints as well as lawsuits from inmates, advocacy organizations and government agencies, judges around the country are intervening on behalf of prisoners, ordering jails and prisons to boost staffing, increase pay and even hire new doctors and nurses. In other cases they have compelled institutions to offer broader ranges of healthcare services to the incarcerated.

Last year [2006], a Michigan federal judge found the state's Department of Corrections in contempt of court, threatened to fine the department $2 million for providing constitutionally inadequate healthcare to state prisoners, and ordered it to hire more physicians at three state prisons near Jackson. U.S.

Mark Taylor, "Prisoners of the System," *Modern Healthcare*, February 19, 2007. Reprinted with permission from Modern Healthcare.

District Judge Richard Enslen ordered the department to hire more nurses, create a staffing plan and make other healthcare improvements.

A federal monitor has overseen healthcare at the Jackson facilities since a consent decree was signed to settle a 1980 class-action civil rights lawsuit. The decree set standards of care that Enslen contended the state has repeatedly failed to achieve.

Judges around the country are intervening on behalf of prisoners, ordering jails and prisons to boost staffing, increase pay and even hire new doctors and nurses.

Some examples:

In August 2006, a mentally ill Michigan prisoner, Timothy Souders, 21, died after being kept naked and shackled to a bed for as long as 17 hours a day. In his 61-page order released in November, Enslen ordered sweeping changes and banned the kinds of restraints used on Souders. He wrote that what a prisoner "does not deserve is a de facto and unauthorized death penalty at the hands of a callous and dysfunctional healthcare system that regularly fails to treat life-threatening illness."

Earlier this month [February 2007], a monitor appointed by a federal judge to oversee improvements in California's correctional healthcare system met with state legislators, warning them that unless action is taken soon, he would seek court orders to mandate improvements. California's projected $1.9 billion prison healthcare budget for 2008 does not include money to build new prison acute-care and mental health hospitals that are needed according to the federal monitor.

The U.S. Justice Department's Civil Rights division concluded in a report last year [2006] that medical and mental healthcare as well as sanitary conditions at the Dallas County (Texas) Jail were inadequate and violated the constitutional rights of the inmates detained there. Among other deficiencies, the office found substandard acute- and chronic-care services; failures to appropriately manage communicable diseases and medication administration; and insufficient staffing, specialty care and training. For each deficiency Assistant Attorney General Wan Kim cited multiple failures of care resulting in harm or death to prisoners.

Some 30 years ago the U.S. Supreme Court created a right for prisoners denied to most other Americans: a constitutional right to healthcare.

Hospitals increasingly are caught in the middle, picking up the tab for uninsured prisoners, such as in Oklahoma City where Oklahoma County rules prevent it from paying for treatment for pre-existing conditions in prisoners, leaving hospitals to provide care for which they're unlikely to be reimbursed. Some hospitals and health systems, such as the 806-bed Parkland Health & Hospital System, Dallas, have contracted to care for county prisoners to varying degrees of success. For-profit companies to which states and municipalities often outsource prison healthcare services also have come under fire for understaffing facilities and skimping on care.

Experts in prison healthcare say solutions to the systemic problems are complex and varied. After all, it's not like government authorities have a choice in providing health benefits to prisoners. Some 30 years ago the U.S. Supreme Court created a right for prisoners denied to most other Americans: a constitutional right to healthcare.

Landmark Case

In that 1976 decision, *Estelle v. Gamble,* a Texas inmate claimed he was subjected to cruel and unusual punishment in violation of the Eighth Amendment to the U.S. Constitution for inadequate treatment received for a back injury he suffered while performing prison work. The high court concluded that inmates must rely on prison authorities to treat medical needs, which would otherwise go unmet and could result in pain and suffering or even a lingering death. "The infliction of such unnecessary suffering is inconsistent with contemporary standards of decency," the U.S. Supreme Court concluded in its 8-1 decision.

The decision sparked dramatic changes in the way healthcare is delivered in prisons and jails around the nation, launching a multibillion-dollar industry. The American Medical Association and the American Bar Association worked to establish a commission to study correctional health services in 1972. They set the first jail standards in 1976 and the first standards for juvenile facilities and prisons in 1979. In 1983, the National Commission on Correctional Health Care was incorporated to accredit correctional healthcare facilities.

The *Gamble* case also triggered waves of litigation by prisoners and prisoner advocacy groups, including the American Civil Liberties Union, which compelled correctional institutions to provide a community standard of healthcare services rivaling and, in some cases, exceeding the coverage that insured Americans enjoy.

B. Jaye Anno, a co-founder of the National Commission and now a Santa Fe, N.M., correctional healthcare consultant, says that at the time of the Supreme Court decision, healthcare in correctional settings was considered a privilege, not a right.

By the early to mid-'90s most jails and prisons boasted respectable healthcare delivery systems.

"Before that if you were a sick prisoner you had to convince a correctional officer of your illness, and if he liked you, he'd take you to the nearest emergency room," Anno recalls. "There were no on-site healthcare delivery systems in prisons.

You were often treated by unlicensed 'inmate nurses.' In those days there were many impaired physicians or doctors with significant restrictions on their licenses who couldn't see patients or get hired elsewhere (other than treating prisoners). The *Gamble* case changed all that."

Anno and her late husband, Chicago attorney Bernard Harrison, another co-founder of the commission, who had been a vice president of the AMA, worked with the association's Jail Project in the early 1970s to study the institutional problems and recommend improvements.

She says by the early to mid-'90s most jails and prisons boasted respectable healthcare delivery systems. Physicians now operate under clinical protocols and guidelines comparable to those outside of prisons and are tightly credentialed. Jail and prison health systems and hospitals are accredited by three national bodies: the National Commission, the American Correctional Association and the Joint Commission.

Litigation forced cities, counties and states to spend large amounts to improve the healthcare offered to prisoners.

Joseph Paris, a physician, former medical director for the Georgia Department of Corrections and prison health consultant, says the Gamble case shook up the national correctional establishment.

"It became quickly apparent that most systems operated well below standards set by the Supreme Court. Litigation became a wave around the country," he says. "The courts maintained oversight of those programs for years after (lawsuits were filed and settlements signed). Standards improved, and correctional healthcare began to resemble the care someone on the outside would receive if that person happened to be well-insured. This provoked a massive improvement in (prison) healthcare."

Paris says the litigation forced cities, counties and states to spend large amounts to improve the healthcare offered to prisoners. He says the cost of providing a "community standard of care" to prisoners comparable with that received by most insured Americans averages about $4,000 per inmate annually. He says that improving quality usually reduces litigation, but doesn't necessarily lower costs. And as government budgets are stretched and the number of uninsured approaches 47 million, he sees little popular support for continued improvements for increasingly costly prison health services.

State prison healthcare spending can vary widely. In 1998, California spent $483 million on prison healthcare for its roughly 157,000 prisoners, just over $3,000 per prisoner annually, or about 13% of its corrections budget. North Dakota spent about $826,000 on its roughly 800 prisoners, or a little more than $1,000 per prisoner, less than 5% of its total corrections budget. That year states spent an average of 12% of their total corrections budgets on prison healthcare, according to a 2001 book by Anno sponsored by the federal National Institute of Corrections, titled *Correctional Health Care: Guidelines for the Management of an Adequate Delivery System.*

'Incarceration Frenzy'

Meanwhile, changes in judicial sentencing rules, an epidemic of drug use and decades of "tough on crime" laws have packed prisons and jails, contributing to overcrowding conditions and quality-of-care problems.

"We are on an incarceration frenzy," says Joel Dvoskin, a psychologist and mental health consultant who teaches at the University of Arizona College of Medicine and is president of the American Psychology-Law Society. "In 1970, there were fewer than 400,000 prisoners and inmates in prisons and jails. Now we're on track to have 2.5 million people behind bars."

"Nobody ever got elected promising to raise taxes," Dvoskin says, noting that courts have pushed state and municipal governments to improve medical and mental health services for prisoners. "We've seen an astonishing difference in the quality of mental health services in prisons since 1976. Litigation is a very bad way to improve things. But the threat of (litigation) is a very good way. Jails are public health outposts. Folks who would be running around infecting people sometimes get treatment in jails they wouldn't or couldn't get in the free world."

The incarcerated include a healthy-size portion of unhealthy patients, a captive population that averages 2.2 million daily.

Between 9 million and 11 million prisoners will be released within a given year, often transmitting infectious diseases they acquired behind bars to the general public and back to prison if they return. But it isn't just the fast-growing number of prisoners causing breakdowns in the prison healthcare system.

Though recent, accurate figures are not available, in 1996 between 12% to 35% of those in the U.S. with communicable diseases passed through jails or prisons, according to the National Commission. In 1997 there were 137,000 cases of sexually transmitted diseases among prisoners and three times that number—about 465,000—among released prisoners. More than one-quarter of inmates have some form of hepatitis, 12,000 have active tuberculosis and 135,000 have tested positive for TB.

While the number of both HIV-infected state and federal prisoners and AIDS-related prisoner deaths dropped for the fifth year in a row in 2004, the percentage of HIV-positive and AIDS patients in prison remains disproportionately high compared with the general population, according to the U.S. Justice Department's Bureau of Justice Statistics.

\ber of HIV-positive inmates decreased 2.6% to
4 from 23,663 in 2003, and down 10.7% from a
⌐ut 25,800 in 1999. AIDS-related deaths dropped
⌐⌐ to 203 in 2004 from 282 in 2003, and the death rate
from AIDS dropped as well. But the number of confirmed
AIDS cases increased 1.4% to 6,027 in 2004 from 5,944 in
2003.

And the rate of AIDS cases among inmates (50 per 10,000
prisoners) remained more than three times higher than the
general population (15 per 10,000 persons). Justice Department statisticians attributed the decrease in AIDS deaths and
HIV infection to the introduction of protease inhibitors and
antiretroviral therapies.

The High Cost of Care

Government studies also indicate that more than 60% of
prison and jail patients have mild or serious mental illnesses
or substance-abuse problems. Those addictions aggravate complex respiratory conditions, infectious diseases and chronic
conditions, such as diabetes and heart disease, prison health
experts say. And the bulk of the cost of caring for them, estimated at between $7 billion and $8 billion annually for all
prisons, is footed by taxpayers whose elected officials never
want to be viewed as soft on crime or generous with benefits
for criminals.

Prisoners typically don't have high-powered lobbyists
pleading their cases, as do seniors, people with disabilities and
patients with cancer and heart disease. Prisoners are disproportionately black and Hispanic, mostly poor and frequently
uneducated, according to federal prison studies and the American Correctional Association.

"We serve the most disenfranchised people in this country," says physician Sergio Rodriguez, until recently the medical director of Cermak Health Services of Cook County (Ill.),
the largest single-site correctional health facility in the coun-

try, which annually provides healthcare services to about 100,000 prisoners at the Cook County Jail.

"They never integrate into the healthcare system outside. We are their primary-care provider. They don't see us as jailers, but as advocates. We are their doctors, sometimes the only ones they ever see."

Rodriguez won't be seeing his prison patients anytime soon. Shortly after *Modern Healthcare* interviewed him for this story, the interim chief of the Cook County Bureau of Health Services fired Rodriguez and four other prison health executives, alleging that they would resist budget-driven changes at Cermak Health Services.

R. Scott Chavez, vice president of the National Commission, says the prison healthcare industry lags behind its "free world" counterpart in a variety of ways, but also suffers from many of the same problems. He says the prison health system is highly fragmented between federal, state, county and city prisons and jails, with little or no communication, little outcomes data or access to information technology and no reliable, current national statistics about the healthcare conditions and status of prisoners.

"We don't have good epidemiological information," Chavez says. "We need, and have recommended to Congress a unified clearinghouse of centralized surveillance. We need better data. One of the major changes we've seen is a great push to apply evidence-based medicine to (correctional) settings. But the public doesn't want to hear about the higher costs of accomplishing that, and institutions are doing more with less."

Prison Inmates Will No Longer Be Segregated by Race

Tanya Schevitz

Tanya Schevitz is a staff writer for the San Francisco Chronicle.

San Quentin State Prison inmate Lexy Good is white, hangs out with whites on the prison exercise yard and must be careful not to associate with blacks and Latinos. No cards, no basketball outside the color lines.

Those are the unwritten inmate rules of prison life. People stick to their own race.

Good, who's doing a short stretch for receiving stolen property, likes it that way. "We segregate amongst ourselves because I'd rather hang out with white people, and blacks would rather hang out with people of their own race," said Good, 33, of Walnut Creek. "Look at suburbia. Look at Oakland. Look at Beverly Hills. People in society self-segregate."

Soon that may change in the prisons. San Quentin and 30 or so other state penal facilities are gearing up to carry out a federal court mediation agreement for integrating double cells and ending the use of race as the sole determining factor in making cell assignments.

Men in California's prisons have long been segregated in cells to quell racial tensions. But Good, along with California's other 155,700 male inmates, may soon be forced to live in a 4-by-9-foot cell with an inmate of a different race.

A 1995 lawsuit filed by a black California inmate, Garrison Johnson, said that the California Department of Corrections' practice of segregating prisoners by race violated his rights. A 2005 ruling by the U.S. Supreme Court led to federal court mediation and the agreement that double cells would be desegregated.

Tanya Schevitz, "Prisons Prepare to Integrate Cellmates," *San Francisco Chronicle*, May 27, 2008, p. A-1. Copyright © 2008 Hearst Communications Inc., Hearst Newspaper Division. Reproduced by permission.

While most inmates and correctional officials agree that it is a noble idea, many fear the worst. "They should be thinking about what kind of war they are going to start," said a San Quentin inmate who identified himself only as S. Styles, 36, of Vallejo. "It is like putting a cat and a dog in a cell together."

Lt. Rudy Luna, assistant to the warden at San Quentin, said there is some concern among prison officials about the change because much of the violence is already based around racial gangs.

State Mandate

"There is always concern, but that is a rule that has been sent down. There are a lot of times we don't like what we have to do," Luna said. "I think we will have a spike in fighting because we have races that don't get along. If it was up to us, we'd keep it the way it is. But it is a state mandate."

While most inmates and correctional officials agree that [desegregation of cells] is a noble idea, many fear the worst.

Among the state's male inmates, about 28.9 percent are black, 39.3 percent are Latino, 25.9 percent are white, and 5.9 percent are classified as other, according to figures from the state Department of Corrections.

"There are a lot of incidents in prison where you have a group of inmates going against another group of inmates," said Terry Thornton, spokeswoman for the California Department of Corrections and Rehabilitation. "You have these groups aligned along race but it is about control. It is about criminal activities." . . .

Interviewing Inmates

In carrying out the plan, prison officials will interview and evaluate each inmate. Department of Corrections officials know some inmates cannot be placed with inmates of other races. But those who are deemed eligible and still refuse will face discipline ranging from loss of privileges to solitary confinement.

Guards and staff have also been undergoing training for the past year on procedures and have been told to be alert for signs of abuse or fighting, Thornton said. "The benefit is for inmates to live how they are supposed to live. It is rehabilitative. This is how we live in the world. It should be the same way in prison too," Thornton said. "It breaks down all of those prejudicial barriers."

The new plan will help the prisons manage the criminal prison gangs, which are divided racially.

Inmate David Johnson said that all the races sit together peacefully in the prison church and they work together with few problems. But he wouldn't socialize with inmates of another race outside of those settings where he is forced to mingle.

Loyal to His Race

"Prison politics" dictate that he stay loyal to his race, Johnson said. And the repercussions for a violation are swift and severe. "You would be taken care of in some way. You could get stabbed or worse," said Johnson, 38, of San Diego. "Whether you agree with the (unwritten) rules or not, you have to follow them."

That's why prison officials said the new plan will help the prisons manage the criminal prison gangs, which are divided racially and strictly control who their members associate with. "Ninety percent of the gang members don't want to be in a gang but they can't get out. But now we are giving them a way out. It will be an excuse for a white to be with a black and a black to be with a white," Luna said.

The race lines are stark throughout the prisons. One recent sunny afternoon on the exercise yard of San Quentin, a group of two dozen or so African American inmates congregated around the basketball court, shooting hoops or just talking. White inmates were in the middle of the yard, playing ping pong or cards. And the Latino inmates were at the far end of the yard where there was some exercise equipment.

The race lines are stark throughout the prisons.

In a nearby courtyard, inmates who had recently arrived sat in small groups, mostly segregated except for those doing an intake exam. Carnell Bradley, 23, Gregory Ealey, 27 and Wayne Griffin, 22, all of Oakland and all black, sat together and agreed that the integration plan is flawed.

'That Is How Jail Is'

"It is going to cause problems. As soon as the cellmates get into a fight, it will become a race against race thing," said Ealey. "It is going to bring everybody into it because that is how jail is. It is just more comfortable being with your own race."

However, experts say it can work. The Texas prison system integrated its cells in the early 1990s and eventually saw a decline in racial tensions, said Professor Jim Marquart, chair of the criminology department at the University of Texas at Dallas, who studied the transition and is advising California during its process.

"The people said, 'It can't be done, you are going to have helter skelter in the prisons.' On the other side, you had people say it can be done. But basically, it was somewhere in between," said Marquart, who authored a report called "The Caged Melting Pot." He said there was a spike in interracial violence at first. But after a while it died down, and the levels of interracial violence are now less than in the general population.

"We are not here to say that everybody is holding hands and singing Kumbaya. There is a lot of hate. There is a lot of animosity. But inmates are intelligent and they want to just do their time and they want to go home," said Marquart. "It worked here. It is an uneasy peace and truce, but it worked. I have ultimate faith in their ability to do it in California."

The Constitution Does Not Prohibit Serving Prisoners Unappetizing Food

Arin Greenwood

Arin Greenwood is a Washington, D.C., attorney and writer whose articles have appeared in many publications.

Nobody thinks prison food is haute cuisine, but could it be so bad it's unconstitutional? The question comes up more often than you might think, and there's one dish in particular that so offends the palates of America's prisoners that it's repeatedly been the subject of lawsuits: Nutraloaf.

Nutraloaf (sometimes called Nutri-loaf, sometimes just "the loaf") is served in state prisons around the country. It's not part of the regular menu but is prescribed for inmates who have misbehaved in various ways—usually by proving untrustworthy with their utensils. The loaf provides a full day's nutrients, and it's finger food—no fork necessary.

Prisoners Have Sued

Prisoners sue over Nutraloaf with some regularity, usually arguing either that their due process rights have been violated (because they are served the punitive loaves without a hearing) or that the dish is so disgusting as to make it cruel and unusual and thus a violation of the Eighth Amendment. Typical of these suits is the 1992 case *LeMaire v. Maass.* Samuel LeMaire slit a man's throat before going to state prison and attacked his prison guards and fellow prisoners with sharpened poles, feces, and a homemade knife once inside. LeMaire was then put in a Nutraloaf-serving disciplinary unit. Among other complaints about the accommodations there, LeMaire

Arin Greenwood, "Taste-Testing Nutraloaf," *Slate*, June 24, 2008. Copyright © Washington Post. Newsweek Interactive Co. LLC. Reproduced by permission of author.

argued that Nutraloaf was cruel and unusual and thus violated his Eighth Amendment rights.

A lower court agreed with LeMaire and ordered the prison to serve him something more delicious. The Ninth Circuit, however, overturned the lower court's decision, holding that while Nutraloaf may be unappetizing, "The Eighth Amendment requires only that prisoners receive food that is adequate to maintain health; it need not be tasty or aesthetically pleasing."

Prisoners in Illinois, Maryland, Nebraska, New York, Pennsylvania, Washington, and West Virginia, among other states, have sued over Nutraloaf or its equivalent. The latest court to hear a Nutraloaf case is the Vermont Supreme Court, where prisoners argued that Vermont's use of the loaf violated their due process rights. (In Vermont, the punishment is one loaf, served at normal meal times, for up to a week.) Oral arguments were heard in March [2008] and a decision is expected to come down by the end of the year. But it doesn't look good for the prisoners. The lawyer representing the prisoners noted that "Nutraloaf has been found to be uniformly unappetizing to everyone who has been served it." To which one justice replied: "Counsel, I've eaten Nutraloaf. And it isn't tasty. But many things I've eaten aren't tasty."

The Eighth Amendment requires only that prisoners receive food that is adequate to maintain health; it need not be tasty or aesthetically pleasing.

Even unsympathetic courts seem willing to concede that Nutraloaf is pretty disgusting, but after reading through the court filings in these cases, I couldn't shake a nagging question—just how bad is it? Nutraloaf is made differently in different prisons. Vermont's penal cookbook calls for a combination of vegetables, beans, bread, cheese, and raisins. I recently spent $15 on a nearly identical dish at a vegan cafe in New

York—and it didn't even have raisins. In a spirit of legal and culinary adventurousness, I decided to make some Nutraloaf of my own.

Taste-Testing Nutraloaf

I chose three test recipes that seemed representative of the various loaves served in prisons across the land: a vegan Nutraloaf from Illinois that is heavy on processed ingredients (and has been the subject of lawsuits); a meat recipe from California that favors fresh, natural ingredients (which has not been challenged in court); and the Nutraloaf from Vermont, the one most recently at issue before a court.

I started with Illinois. I mixed canned spinach in with baked beans, tomato paste, margarine, applesauce, bread crumbs, and garlic powder. Together the ingredients became a thick, odorous, brown paste, which I spread into a loaf pan and put in the oven. After 40 minutes, I took the loaf out of the oven and sliced some off. It was dense and dry and tasted like falafel gone wrong. But instead of it making me feel pleasantly sated like falafel does, even the small test slice I sampled gave me a stomachache.

Even unsympathetic courts seem willing to concede that Nutraloaf is pretty disgusting.

I cooked up Vermont next, wondering what I'd gotten myself into. Vermont was like Illinois but with raisins and nondairy cheese. I'm a vegetarian, so my sister-in-law Lori volunteered to cook the California loaf, which includes ground beef. As she mixed up the chopped cabbage, diced carrots, cubed potatoes, whole wheat flour, and beans, I realized that what she was making looked delicious, at least compared with the first two loaves. Lori kindly offered to make two California loaves—one with meat and one without, our only deviation from the Nutraloaf recipes.

To test the loaves, I invited friends and relatives over for what I promised would be an educational dinner party. This being Washington, D.C., more than half the adults were lawyers, which I thought gave our experiment a nice jurisprudential twist. To keep the Nutraloaf test authentic, I mandated that my guests eat with their hands; plus, after sneaking in that taste of Illinois earlier in the day, I was worried someone might stab *me* if I let them use utensils.

I thought I'd start out easy with the loaf that hasn't inspired a lawsuit—yet. California looked nice on the plate, though it didn't quite hold together as a loaf. I picked some off my plate with my fingers. It tasted a bit like vegetarian chili. Not bad. My cousin Steve, a mortgage broker who had sampled the California loaf with meat, disagreed. "It's what you imagine Alpo tastes like," he said. Lori said she liked it and said she'd even consider making it again, though she'd use more spices. Lee, a lawyer and her husband, asked her not to.

Next came Illinois. I couldn't bear to try another piece; the others were divided about whether it was cruel or merely unusual. Lee described Illinois as "absolutely detestable." David, a lawyer, liked it and willingly ate a second piece. Steve summed up Illinois generously: "I think if you like baked beans, you like Illinois. I like baked beans. I wouldn't think it's fair to sue anyone over it."

Courts have nearly all found that prison food can be unappetizing, cold, and even contain foreign objects, and still not be unconstitutional.

Last came Vermont. It looked the best of the three—it was moist—and the nondairy cheese and canned carrots gave it a fetching orange color. But it tasted terrible. Mike, a computer guy at NASA, said the raisins were disconcerting; you couldn't tell if they were supposed to be in there or not. Steve said he hated it, but it wasn't the worst thing he'd ever eaten. I asked him what was the worst thing he'd ever eaten. "Cat," he said. "But I didn't know it was cat." David, meanwhile, helped himself to another slice of Illinois, a decision he later came to regret. "The third slice sits a little heavy," he said.

As the night went on, and wine washed away the taste of loaves, we discussed the Eighth Amendment and how bad food would actually have to be in order to be unconstitutional. Kim, a lawyer who works in asylum law and knows a human rights violation when she sees one, said the loaves would have to be extremely bad—considerably worse than any of the food we'd just eaten. Courts have nearly all found that prison food can be unappetizing, cold, and even contain foreign objects, and still not be unconstitutional.

Inmates hoping for relief from the courts for their Nutraloaf punishments aren't likely to get it from the courts. They won't likely get it from the prison cooks, either. When the Vermont prison's lawyer was asked during oral arguments why Nutraloaf couldn't be made more appetizing, he answered that if it were tastier, then prisoners would act up for the privilege of getting Nutraloaf. Hardly a ringing endorsement for the rest of the prison menu.

Imprisonment Is Not Supposed To Be Enjoyable

James H. Lilley

James Lilley is a former Marine and highly decorated twenty-five year veteran of the Howard County, Maryland Police Department. His awards include the Medal of Valor, four Bronze Stars, four Unit Citations and the governor's citation. Jim was selected as the 2008 Police-Writers.com Author of the year, was awarded Second Place in the 2009 Police-Writers.com short story contest, and received an Honorable Mention for his book, The Eyes of the Hunter, *in the New England Book Festival.* The Eyes of the Hunter *has also been adopted by Johns Hopkins University as required reading in the Master of Science in Intelligence Analysis program. Jim is also a lecturer at Johns Hopkins.*

The Van Zandt County, Texas Detention Center in Canton, Texas, has taken a page from the "Prison Handbook" of Sheriff Joe Arpaio of Maricopa County, Arizona. That's right, the new standard in fashion wear for prisoners in the Van Zandt County Slammer is PINK. And, prisoners interviewed by CNN News, openly expressed their embarrassment over their new garb, and vowed to never return to the jail—even if it meant never committing another crime.

The Tent City Jail

Sheriff Arpaio believes jails and prisons shouldn't be set up as the Ritz/Carlton for those who break the law. Prison wear for inmates at the Maricopa County Jail, which is a Tent City Jail created by the Sheriff, became pink from head to toe—under-

James H. Lilley, "Prison Inmates Pretty in Pink," *Baltimore Reporter*, January 13, 2008. Reproduced by permission of the author.

wear and socks included. He created chain gangs, so the mates could work on county and city projects at no cost to the taxpayers. He then established a chain gang for women so he wouldn't be sued for discrimination. He put an end to pornographic magazines and smoking, took away the weights, and allows only "G" rated movies to be shown. He stopped Cable TV, until he discovered that a Federal Court Order required Cable TV for jails. He turned the Cable TV on again, but it only receives the Disney Channel and the Weather Channel. Someone asked the Sheriff, "Why the weather channel?" He replied, "So they'll know how hot it's gonna be while they're working on my chain gang."

When temperatures soared to over 130 degrees in the Tent City Jail, Sheriff Joe Arpaio allowed the inmates to strip down to their pink boxer shorts. One tent city inmate complained, "It feels like we're in a Furnace. It's inhumane." Sheriff Arpaio offered no sympathy for his plight. He said, "It's 120 degrees in Iraq, and our soldiers are living in tents too. And, they have to wear full battle gear, but they didn't commit any crimes. So shut your damned mouth."

Sheriff Arpaio believes jails and prisons shouldn't be set up as the Ritz/Carlton for those who break the law.

He also cut off all coffee at the jail, because it has no nutritional value. When the inmates complained about the loss of their coffee, he simply said, "If you don't like it, don't come back."

He bought the Newt Gingrich [former history professor and Republican congressman] lecture series on tape, and piped it into the jail. A reporter asked if he had any lecture series by a Democrat. He replied that a democratic lecture series might explain why a lot of the inmates were in his jails in the first place.

heriff Arpaio has also found ways to save the
ins of dollars. Maricopa County was spending
ars a year dealing with stray animals, such as
cats and dogs. He offered to take over the department, and
the County Supervisors agreed. All animal shelters are now
staffed and operated by prisoners. They feed and care for the
strays, and every animal is taken out and walked twice daily.
He now has prisoners who have become experts in animal nu-
trition and behavior, and these same inmates provide classes
for anyone adopting animals. He has taken some stray dogs
off the streets, put them under the care of prisoners, and had
them place in dog shows. The entire program now operates
on a budget under 3 million dollars a year.

---

*It would be very difficult trying to play the role of a ma-
cho gang-banger . . . while standing around in pink socks
and underwear.*

If every state across the nation would put one program,
such as this, in operation at a saving of over 15 million dollars
annually, the taxpayers would save over 7.5 billion dollars.

The Maricopa County Jail has a large farm, which was do-
nated to the county years ago, where inmates can work. They
grow most of their own fresh vegetables and food, doing the
work and harvesting by hand. There is also a fairly good-sized
hog farm, which provides meat and fertilizer. The fertilizer is
used to fertilize the Christmas trees at a nursery where the
prisoners work, and you can buy a living Christmas tree for as
little as six dollars, and replant it later.

Is there any reason why similar programs cannot be established and utilized throughout the nation's correctional system? Again, there would be the saving of millions of dollars in
taxes, tax dollars spent on purchasing foods that could be
grown for use within the penal system. Indeed, there may be

arguments that certain climates in various states v
hibit such programs, and some locations would
such programs at all. But, vegetables grown in Calif
Arizona can be shipped to Maine, and livestock i ....u in
Texas could be used to feed inmates in Seattle and New York.
Yes, a cooperative effort nationwide to save the taxpayer
money. It also occupies and teaches those who participate in
the programs a valuable skill, and surely it wouldn't damage
their self-esteem. In the end, the hard work and accomplish-
ment would tend to bolster an inmate's self-worth.

Sheriff Joe Arpaio continues to be reelected to office. . . .
But, he's not a favorite with the ACLU [American Civil Liberties Union]. He's taken another initiative, painting all of his
buses and vehicles with a mural, which have a special hotline
telephone number for calling and reporting illegal allens. He
wasn't satisfied with the job being done by Immigration and
Customs, and had 40 deputies trained specifically for enforcing immigration laws. In addition to his hotline to report illegal aliens, he purchased four new buses to haul them back to
the border.

> If our politicians, corrections and law enforcement offi-
> cials are as eager to find solutions to the crime problem,
> as they claim they are, power struggles and egos need to
> be put aside.

Though in the eyes of the bleeding hearts, the ACLU, and
certainly a few of our "esteemed" politicians, Sheriff Joe Arpaio might be a rogue, or seem out of control with his programs. Yet, with less than 50% of his prisoners returning to
jail, he must be doing something right.

Mandated Pink Prison Garb

If wearing pink, in only two locations around the country, has
stimulated dozens of inmates to want to change their evil

ways, it seems that pink should become the new jailhouse fashion frenzy across the country. To some it might seem far-fetched, but what's the harm in testing Sheriff Arpaio's methods? Imagine the savings in tax dollars if pink inspired a half-dozen inmates from every correctional facility around the country to walk the straight and narrow. And, with nation-wide publicity, could it have an effect on others who are already engaging in a life of crime, and the wannabe thugs? Let's face it, wearing pink doesn't do much to enhance the tough guy image. And, it would be very difficult trying to play the role of a macho gang-banger, even with head to toe tattoos, while standing around in pink socks and underwear.

We've heard law enforcement and elected officials promise hard-line tactics to enforce the laws and rid our streets of crime. Yet, in spite of political bravado, often times complete with fist pumping, crime hasn't been swept from the streets. Screams for stricter laws, more stringent sentencing guidelines, and the never-ending cries to ban firearms have filled the news for years, and criminals still freely prowl the streets of America. But, could something as simple as mandating that inmates across America will henceforth wear pink, be the solution to our crime problem? And, studies have shown that the color pink does indeed have a very calming effect.

Any endeavor of this magnitude would require total cooperation on the federal, state and local level in our correctional system. Yet, there is no reason why cooperation cannot be attained—unless egos get in the way. If our politicians, corrections and law enforcement officials are as eager to find solutions to the crime problem, as they claim they are, power struggles and egos need to be put aside. Sheriff Arpaio seems to have found a workable solution, which includes inmates working to provide goods and services for themselves and others. Most other programs, including gun buy backs, have failed miserably. Why not follow Sheriff Joe Arpaio's lead and test his methods? We have nothing to lose, but much to gain if it works around the nation.

A project of this dimension would certainly bring the ACLU, and the bleeding hearts charging to the courts to scream rights violations, cruel and unusual punishment, and anything else they could dream up. But, this is the time the courts would have to be unwavering in their support of the program, and suggest the ACLU and bleeding hearts pack their bags for Iran, or North Korea.

Any such undertaking shouldn't be done quietly. It should be publicized, on billboard advertisements, in television commercials, and movie trailers. Publicity showing an inmate behind bars, wearing pink with a caption of, "If you think you're tough enough to commit the crime, be sure you're tough enough to wear this, while doing your time," might create a remarkable impression.

Imagine criminals and wannabe thugs, around the country asking themselves, "Do I really wanna look pretty in pink?"

CHAPTER 3

What Can Be Done About Prison Overcrowding?

Chapter Preface

If there is anything about which all observers of prisons agree, it is that they are currently overcrowded. In California, for example, as of early 2009 there are 158,000 inmates packed into prisons designed to hold 84,000. Nearly 14,000 inmates are sleeping in three-tier bunks set up in converted classrooms or gyms, so close together that each prisoner has only six square feet of living space. In some states, prisoners are sleeping in hallways or on the floor. Prisons all over the nation are bursting at the seams, and the number of people incarcerated is increasing faster than new prisons can be built, even where taxpayers have agreed to fund them.

In some states taxpayers appear willing to go on paying for more prisons, even though most experts believe the money could be spent more effectively on alternatives to prison and on supervision of criminals on probation or parole. But many people believe the only realistic solution is the repeal of mandatory sentencing and "truth in sentencing" (elimination of parole) laws, which, along with the America's war on drugs, are generally acknowledged to be the main causes of the prison population explosion. Some also believe nonviolent offenders should not be taking up prison space.

Such policy changes, however, are proposals for the long term, whereas overcrowding needs to be relieved right away. If all else fails, it will be necessary to let some criminals out of prison. This already is happening in a few places, and in February 2009 a panel of federal judges tentatively ordered California to release more than 50,000 prisoners because of unhealthy living conditions and a lack of medical care serious enough to be ruled unconstitutional.

An increasingly common way of gaining prison space is to use private prisons. There are companies that specialize in prison operation, and supporters of this option believe private prisons are not only run more efficiently than government-run ones, but that they take better care of inmates. Opponents, on the other hand, say private prison companies cut corners to make a higher profit; there have been many lawsuits, especially related to inadequate medical care. However, because private prison companies must compete for contracts, they can be called to account for mismanagement and can lose contracts if their performance is poor.

Private prison companies also say that using them eliminates unethical practices of government prisons, such as hiring workers on the basis of political patronage. But some private prisons are nevertheless involved in corruption. In February 2009 two Pennsylvania judges were convicted of receiving kickbacks from private detention facilities to which they had sent hundreds of teenagers for trivial offenses that did not merit imprisonment. Keeping people in prison is very costly for taxpayers, but to the prison industry—not only private prisons but the suppliers of government-run ones—prisoners mean profits.

The most promising way of reducing prison overcrowding may be to use advanced technology, such as global positioning system (GPS) tracking, to electronically monitor offenders sentenced to supervision on the outside. In the future, the cost of such technology may decrease, and it may become possible to effectively control nonviolent criminals without locking them up.

Many States Are Releasing Prisoners Early

Keith B. Richburg and Ashley Surdin

Keith B. Richburg and Ashley Surdin are staff writers for the Washington Post.

Reversing decades of tough-on-crime policies, including mandatory minimum prison sentences for some drug offenders, many cash-strapped states are embracing a view once dismissed as dangerously naive: It costs far less to let some felons go free than to keep them locked up.

It is a theory that has long been pushed by criminal justice advocates and liberal politicians—that some felons, particularly those convicted of minor drug offenses, would be better served by treatment, parole or early release for good behavior. But the states' conversion to that view has less to do with a change of heart on crime than with stark fiscal realities. At a time of shrinking resources, prisons are eating up an increasing share of many state budgets.

"It's the fiscal stuff that's driving it," said Marc Mauer, executive director of the Sentencing Project, a Washington-based group that advocates for more lenient sentencing. "Do you want to build prisons or do you want to build colleges? If you're a governor, it's kind of come to that choice right now."

Some felons, particularly those convicted of minor drug offenses, would be better served by treatment, parole or early release for good behavior.

Mauer and other observers point to a number of recent actions, some from states facing huge budget shortfalls, some not, but still worried about exploding costs.

Keith B. Richburg and Ashley Surdin, "Fiscal Pressures Lead Some States to Free Inmates Early," *Washington Post*, May 5, 2008, p. A01. Copyright © 2008, The Washington Post. Reprinted with permission.

- To ease the overcrowding and save California about $1.1 billion over two years, Gov. Arnold Schwarzenegger (R) has proposed freeing about 22,000 prisoners convicted of nonviolent, nonsexual offenses 20 months earlier than their scheduled release dates. He also wants to place them on unsupervised parole, saving the state the cost of having all parolees assigned to an agent.

- Lawmakers in Providence, R.I., approved an expansion last week [May 2008] of the state's "good time" early-release rules to cover more inmates serving shorter sentences. The new rules, which will put more inmates under post-prison supervision, are expected to save Rhode Island an estimated $8 billion over five years.

- In Kentucky, where 22,000 state inmates are housed in county prisons and private facilities, lawmakers agreed to allow certain nonviolent, nonsexual offenders to serve up to 180 days of their sentences at home, and to make it easier for prisoners to earn credit for good behavior. The move could save the state, which is facing a $900 million deficit over the next two years, as much as $30 million.

- In Mississippi, where the prison population has doubled during the past dozen years to 22,600, Gov. Haley Barbour (R) has signed into law two measures that will reduce it: One to let certain nonviolent offenders go free after serving 25 percent of their sentences, and the other to release some terminally ill inmates.

- South Carolina, meanwhile, is looking to abolish parole, in part to slow the growth of its prison population since there would be fewer people returned to prison for parole violations.

Opposition to Early Release

Proposals to free prisoners are still met with opposition, particularly from law enforcement officials who fear that a flood of released felons could return to their communities, and from victims groups that worry that justice is being sacrificed for budgetary concerns.

The California plan has drawn criticism from the Legislative Analyst's Office, the state's nonpartisan fiscal adviser, which warned that 63,000 mid-level offenders would "effectively go unpunished, serving little or no prison time" and would not have active supervision.

The proposal also worries local governments and police in California, particularly in Los Angeles County—home to the nation's largest prison system, which supplies about a third of the state's prison population. "It's kind of like the volcano has erupted," County Sheriff Lee Baca said. "To let out 63,000 prisoners on summary parole—which means no parole—is not good policy."

Bob Pack, 52, of Danville, Calif., is particularly disturbed by the prospect of softer punishment for those convicted of drunken driving. In 2003, Pack's two children—Troy, 10, and Alana, 7—were struck and killed when a drunk driver's car jumped a curb and ran onto a neighborhood sidewalk. The driver had three prior drunken-driving convictions.

Proposals to free prisoners are still met with opposition, particularly from law enforcement officials who fear that a flood of released felons could return to their communities.

Said Pack: "I guarantee you that if this program is fulfilled, somewhere down the road—it could be three months or a year—there's going to be a family in court over the death of a loved one, because of someone who got out early."

Pressure to Cut Costs

But for now, state officials are finding themselves under mounting pressure to cut costs and are looking at their rising prison population.

Between 1987 and last year, states increased their higher education spending by 21 percent, in inflation-adjusted dollars, according to the Pew Center on the States. During the same period, spending on corrections jumped by 127 percent.

In the Northeastern states, according to the Pew report, prison spending over the past 20 years has risen 61 percent, while higher education spending has declined by 5.5 percent.

California—which has the country's worst fiscal crisis, with a potential shortfall of $20 billion—has seen its prison-related spending swell to $10.4 billion for the 2008–2009 fiscal year. About 170,000 inmates are packed into California's 33 prisons, which were designed to hold 100,000. About 15,000 prisoners are being housed in emergency beds, in converted classrooms and gymnasiums.

Rhode Island's prison population peaked and its 4,000-inmate prison capacity was exceeded in recent years, prompting a lawsuit and a court settlement. "The soaring inmate census has created a crisis here," said Ashbel T. Wall, the state's corrections director. "We've been busting the budget continuously. . . . Our prisons have been packed."

New Jersey is one state making changes out of a desire for more efficiency. Gov. Jon S. Corzine (D) is proposing legislation to expand drug courts to channel more nonviolent, first-time drug offenders into treatment instead of prisons, and also to expand supervised parole. Another proposal would change the parole policy so parolees were not automatically returned to prison for minor drug offenses, said Lilo Stainton, the governor's spokeswoman.

She said that in New Jersey's case, the changes are not budget-driven. "We think this is a more humane and sensible way to treat people," she said.

Michigan is grappling with a massive prison population, mainly because "truth in sentencing" rules make the state less generous about granting paroles. Michigan's incarceration rate is 47 percent higher than that of the other Great Lakes states, according to experts.

Michigan has become one of the few states that actually spend more on prisons than on higher education—about $2 billion for prisons, and $1.9 billion in state aid to its 15 public universities and 28 community colleges. "It's insane," said Barbara Levine of the Citizens Alliance on Prisons and Public Spending in Lansing. "The governor is always talking about how we need to be high tech. But these days, the best career opportunity is to get a job as a prison guard."

In fact, according to Thomas Clay, a prisons and budget expert with Michigan's nonprofit Citizens Research Council, the state government employed 70,000 people in 1980, including 5,000 working for the prisons system. Today, the number of state workers has dropped to 54,000, but 17,000 work for the prisons.

"You've got two decades of failed policies," said Laura Sager a consultant in Michigan for Families Against Mandatory Minimums. She said mandatory sentencing laws and tough penalties for drug offenses in the 1980s "bloated prisons and prison populations, and the taxpayer is paying a very high price."

Now with states struggling with budget deficits, she said, "you have pressures that make it palatable to take a second look."

A Federal Court May Rule that California's Prison Population Must Be Reduced

Don Thompson

Don Thompson is a writer for the Associated Press.

Over the past three decades, California lawmakers and voters have sought to combat crime with an ever-expanding list of sentencing laws, adding years to inmates' terms and returning parolees to prison more often.

That get-tough approach has led to a ballooning prison population with unintended consequences—prisons commanding an ever larger share of the state's budget and unconstitutional conditions for inmates.

The federal courts have found that the prison system's delivery of health and mental health care, for example, is so negligent that it's a direct cause of inmate deaths.

The state's day of reckoning for its years of prison overcrowding is expected to come this week [November 2008] in a federal courtroom in San Francisco.

A special three-judge panel reconvenes Tuesday and is prepared to decide whether crowding has become so bad that inmates cannot receive proper care. If they do, a case rooted in several court challenges dating back more than two decades will move to a second phase.

In that phase, the judicial panel will decide if lowering the inmate population is the only way to fix the problems.

That could result in an order to release tens of thousands of California inmates before their terms are finished, a move

Don Thompson, "Federal Judges to Rule on California Prison Crowding," *Associated Press*, November 30, 2008. Copyright © 2008 Associated Press. All rights reserved. This material may not be published, broadcasted, rewritten, or redistributed. Reproduced by permission.

Gov. Arnold Schwarzenegger and Republican lawmakers say would endanger public safety.

"The time has come: The extreme, pervasive and long-lasting overcrowding in California prisons must be addressed," attorney Michael Bien, representing inmates, told the judges during the opening of the trial.

Bien and other civil rights attorneys want the panel to order the prison population cut from 156,300 inmates to about 110,000. That still would be above the capacity of California's 33 state prisons, which were designed to hold fewer than 100,000 inmates.

The prison system's delivery of health and mental health care . . . is so negligent that it's a direct cause of inmate deaths.

To relieve some of the crowding, state corrections officials have transferred nearly 6,000 inmates to privately run prisons out of state and have another 11,000 living in conservation camps or private prisons within California.

The overcrowding is apparent in many prisons. Nearly 14,000 inmates sleep in three-level bunk beds in converted gymnasiums and classrooms. The arrangement gives each inmate about six square feet of living space while increasing the risk of violence and the spread of disease, according to testimony from prison guards.

Some inmates are forced to use water stored in garbage cans to bathe because there are too few showers.

Sick inmates can wait in line for hours to receive medical care, while the mentally ill can wait more than a year for a bed in a treatment unit. The state's inmate suicide rate is double the national average, yet suicidal inmates are held for hours in cages the size of telephone booths because there aren't enough crisis cells.

Two of the three judges hearing the case previously ruled that the state is violating inmates' constitutional rights by providing such poor medical and mental health care.

Jeffrey Beard, secretary of the Pennsylvania Department of Corrections, blamed California's adoption of tough drug laws and three-strikes sentencing laws since the 1970s. The state has added more than 1,000 felony sentencing laws during the past 30 years, and its criminal code gives judges little leeway in deciding punishments.

Nearly 14,000 inmates sleep in three-level bunk beds in converted gymnasiums and classrooms. The arrangement gives each inmate about six square feet of living space.

"They went from being one of the most progressive systems in the country to one of the most overcrowded," Beard testified. "California has this problem that has just been going on for years and years and years, and nobody seems to be willing to step up to the plate and fix the problem."

Most inmates live in prisons with populations the size of small towns. Nearly half the prisons hold 5,000 prisoners or more, while nine exceed 4,000 inmates. Beard said the limit should be 3,300.

The administration argues that conditions are improving, in part because of the out-of-state transfers and because the state is spending more on medical and mental health care.

It will spend $2.2 billion this year to treat, house and guard physically and mentally ill inmates, a 550 percent increase since 1995. The prison's population grew about 30 percent during the same period. Annual health care spending has increased from $2,714 per inmate in 1995 to $13,778 this year, according to the state Department of Finance.

Administration lawyers credited a court-appointed receiver's oversight of inmate health care for many of the recent, if costly, improvements. But the administration is fighting the receiver's demand for an additional $8 billion to build seven inmate medical and mental health centers at a time when the state faces an $11.2 billion budget deficit.

Schwarzenegger and Republican state lawmakers promise an appeal directly to the U.S. Supreme Court if they lose the case.

The state is trying to focus the judges' attention on the consequences of ordering prisoners freed before they complete their full sentences.

"Releasing 50,000 inmates to the streets is obviously a public safety risk and it doesn't fix the problem," Corrections Secretary Matthew Cate said in an interview. "There are still underlying problems and we want to fix them. Early release, though, isn't the way to do that."

The judges are acting for the first time under the federal Prison Litigation Reform Act of 1995. The act requires the judges to initially find that crowding is the main cause of substandard conditions, a ruling they are likely to make this week.

They then can order inmates released only if they find there are no other options for improving care. The judges hope to complete the second phase of the trial by Christmas.

"No one's on the same track as California at this point," said Amy Fettig, a prison lawyer with the American Civil Liberties Union. "It tells you they're in deep, deep trouble."

Private Prisons Increase Capacity, Save Money, and Improve Services

Nathan A. Benefield

Nathan A. Benefield is director of policy research with the Commonwealth Foundation, a research and educational organization based in Harrisburg, Pennsylvania.

There are three types of privatization within prisons and correctional institutions in the US. The first involves contracting out food service, medical services, job training, alcohol and drug rehabilitation, and the like. The second involves publicly owned prisons, which contract out the management to a private firm. The final type of privatization involves fully privatized prisons—both owned and operated by a private firm—which contracts with governments for the care of prisoners.

Pennsylvania House Bill 1469 would only address (that is, prohibit) the third type, i.e. fully private prisons, so I will limit my testimony to privately run prisons, and not address issues of contracting out services.

We believe HB 1469 is a misguided attempt to—well I'm not really sure what HB 1469 is attempting to do, other than deprive elected officials of a good government management tool. Pennsylvania faces a prison crunch, as we expect far greater demands for prison space than we currently have available. Private prisons can help meet this need. Studies demonstrate that private prisons are much more efficient than government-run prisons, and typically save taxpayers 10–15% in per-prisoner costs. Studies also show that private prisons

Nathan A. Benefield, "Private Prisons Increase Capacity, Save Money, Improve Services," *Testimony to the Pennsylvania House Labor Relations Committee*, October 24, 2007. Reproduced by permission of the author.

typically provide better quality service and lower incidents of violence than government run prisons.

Pennsylvania's correctional facilities are in crisis. A growing—and aging—prison population is putting a strain on the budget. In December 2006, the state housed 44,365 prisoners, despite an operational bed capacity of only 39,284, and annual admissions to Pennsylvania's state prisons have increased 53% since 2000 with no indication of abatement. The Pennsylvania Department of Corrections anticipates accommodating 51,596 prisoners by the close of the year 2011—with an estimated 42,851 beds. This would entail operating at 120% capacity.

Studies demonstrate that private prisons are much more efficient than government-run prisons.

At $93.21 per inmate per day, Pennsylvania's prisons are also among the nation's most costly facilities. Pennsylvania currently spends $1.6 billion on corrections annually, an increase of 55% (24% after adjusting for inflation) in the last ten years. The anticipated growth in prison population will add almost $250 million to that cost—assuming per inmate costs remain constant. The Commonwealth faces a looming prison crisis, and the privatization of prison construction, services and management, offers a cost-effective solution to these pressing concerns.

Prison Privatization Is Not New

Critics of prison privatization often call private correctional facilities risky, unproven, or experimental. Yet private prisons operate successfully across the US. Nationally, over 107,000 federal and state prisoners—about 7% of the inmate population—were housed in private facilities in 2005 (an additional 73,000 inmates were held in privately-run local jails). Privately-operated prisons are the most common in the south and west, with five western states—New Mexico (43.3%), Wyoming (41.3%), Hawaii (30.9%), Alaska (28.4%) and Montana (25.5%)—housing more than a quarter of their inmates in private facilities.

Currently, Pennsylvania has only one privately-run prison facility—the Monshannon Valley Correctional Center. But the vast experience of other states with private prisons should serve as case studies for how Pennsylvania can lower costs and provide higher quality services, while also meeting the future demand for correctional services.

By expanding competition, Pennsylvanians can expect anywhere from 5 to 20% savings in per-prisoner costs from private facilities. A wealth of studies . . . find significant cost-savings of prison privatization, most frequently in the range of 10–15% savings.

Private prisons operate successfully across the U.S.

Additionally, states that have introduced privatization in prisons have seen slower rates of growth in correctional costs. A 2003 study found that states with 20% of prisoners in private facilities saw per-prisoner cost grow 5.9% from 1999 to 2001, versus 18.9% in states with no private facilities (states falling in the middle in private prisoners also ranked in the middle in rate of cost growth).

Based on these findings, if Pennsylvania were to place 30% of inmates in private facilities, taxpayers could save upwards of $100 million annually, with higher expected savings in the future.

Private Prisons Offer Higher-Quality Care

Critics of private prisons often allege that privatization leads to lower service quality and endangers public safety. In fact, the opposite appears to be true. While some private prisons have experienced problems, not unlike government-run prisons, on the whole, private prisons have a *better record* of performance than do government-run facilities.

In the private sector, prison management and staff are held accountable for a failure to perform.

Private prisons have many institutional, contractual and legal safeguards to ensure quality, and contractors have compiled an enviable record of providing secure, safe, humane and well-run correctional facilities. Privately-managed correctional facilities have contractual requirements and inherent financial incentives to maintain order and security, provide educational and rehabilitation programs, and respect inmates' civil liberties. A private prison that fails to provide an adequate level of service is likely to suffer contract revocation or the threat thereof, which adversely affects the corporation's ability to offer its services elsewhere and survive among it competitors.

All prisons—public and private—must deal with inmate fights, rapes and attacks on guards. But in the private sector, prison management and staff are held accountable for a failure to perform. The state can terminate a contract with a private prison for mismanagement; private managers and staff are much more likely to face penalties, or be fired, than are government workers; and private companies may go out of business if they don't perform adequately. When is the last time a government-run prison was shut down because of rioting, abuse, poor care, etc.?

But the performance of private prisons is not merely conjecture or theoretical—we have evidence from 34 states. Many studies show private prisons outperforming state-run facilities on quality and performance indicators. A review of prison performance studies found that nine out of the ten rigorous studies of quality found higher quality of service in private prisons, as did most of the less rigorous studies.

The Arizona Department of Corrections reported that private prisons outperformed state-run institutions across the board in safety of the public, staff, and inmates and compliance with professional standards. A University of Florida comparative analysis found significantly lower recidivism rates among comparable inmates released from private prisons. An Urban Institute study reported that inmates and staff alike rated services and programs offered by private facilities as superior to those available in state-run prisons, and found fewer escapes and disturbances at private prisons.

A survey of inmates in Tennessee's Silverdale Detention Center provides further evidence of the ability of private management to substantially improve service quality. Inmates rated the facility highly on most issues, almost invariably better than the facility under previous management, leading the author of the study to conclude that "the evidence is overwhelming that the private takeover of Silverdale has resulted in substantial improvements in the institution's physical conditions and upkeep, as well as several critical areas of inmate service and institutional procedure."

Many studies show private prisons outperforming state-run facilities on quality and performance indicators.

A Bureau of Justice Assistance study found that private prisons have slightly higher rates of assault on inmate and staff, but substantially lower rates of riots and inmate death. . . .

It is also useful to note that private corrections facilities are more than four times more likely than state-run prisons to obtain accreditation with the American Correctional Association, certifying compliance with that organization's standards for quality of operation, management, and maintenance. Part of this discrepancy may be related to private prisons' need to demonstrate quality, whereas public prisons face no such scrutiny.

Prison Privatization Does Not Mean Lost Jobs

While the impact of prison privatization on prisoners and taxpayers are the focus of this testimony—and should be the primary focus of policy makers—unions and employees of public prisons tend to be those objecting most to prison privatization.

An analysis by the Reason Foundation indicates that privatization of existing prison results in a 93% retention of employees, and often involve mitigating the impact of those laid off (often with early retirement options). Much of the employment impact is controlled by a contract between the state and a private provider.

Furthermore, private prisons typically offer comparable compensation. These usually involve defined contribution 401(k) [retirement] plans that may be as generous as traditional defined benefit pensions. Private prisons also frequently offer employees stock options, to take some ownership in the company—this should be viewed both in the light of employee benefits and incentive for quality assurance.

Finally, it should be noted that given Pennsylvania's need for new prison capacity, prison privatization is most likely to be in the form of new capacity. Thus, privatized prisons would likely be *additions to* current state prisons, rather than *replacements for* state prisons. Thus, the State Corrections Officers Association should have no fear of fewer prison jobs, AFSCME [the American Federation of State, County, and Municipal Employees] should have no worries of less union dues, and lawmakers need not to worry about losing control.

In short, private prisons allow Pennsylvania to address its growing need for corrections facilities, at a lower cost to tax-payers, while providing as good or better quality of service as existing state facilities.

Private Prisons Can Ease Overcrowding But May Be Flawed

William Bender

William Bender is a reporter for the Philadelphia Daily News.

At one end of Delaware County's rekindled debate over prison privatization, you'll find Wally Nunn, a tough-talking fiscal hawk and former county councilman. At the other, Fay Kallenbach, a bereaved mother. The George W. Hill Correctional Facility is ground zero.

Nunn led the 1995 effort to privatize the county jail, outsourcing its operation to the GEO Group, a multinational corrections corporation. He stands by his decision today, saying the move cut government waste and saved taxpayers millions of dollars—including the more than $30 million the county saved by hiring GEO, then called Wackenhut Corrections Corp., to build the current prison in 1998. "It's a success right there, by definition," Nunn said.

Fay Kallenbach has a different perspective. She says privatizing the prison has put inmates in the care of a money-hungry "machine" that cuts corners anywhere it can. Her son, comedian Kenneth Keith Kallenbach, died in April of complications from cystic fibrosis while in prison custody. She says he didn't receive the crucial treatment that had kept him alive for 39 years. "They definitely killed my son," she said of Florida-based GEO.

The deep philosophical divide between Kallenbach and Nunn is typical when it comes to prison privatization, a love-it-or-hate-it concept that pits labor unions against politicians and corporate leaders against inmate-advocacy groups.

William Bender, "Privatized Jail: Weighing the Pros and Cons," *Philadelphia Daily News*, December 22, 2008. Copyright © 2008 Philly Online, LLC. All rights reserved. Reproduced by permission.

Regardless, if Nunn is considered Delaware County's "father of privatization," his first born remains an only child in Pennsylvania—and there have been some growing pains lately. In the 12 years since the county handed the jailhouse keys to GEO, no other county in the state has followed its lead. Now, the company is terminating its $40-million-a-year contract there, ridden out of town by an onslaught of lawsuits and inadequate profits. A new firm takes over on New Year's Day [2009].

Privatizing ... has put inmates in the care of a money-hungry "machine" that cuts corners anywhere it can.

All About the Money

Prison Superintendent John Reilly Jr. oversees GEO's performance at the 1,883-bed lockup in Thornton, and he doesn't shy away from discussing the good, the bad and the ugly. There has been plenty of each, from huge cost savings and indemnification from civil-rights lawsuits, to filthy showers and dead inmates.

The cost of operating the prison—nearly $45 million when you factor in the superintendent and his staff—is the single largest expenditure of county tax dollars in the budget. It is expected to eat up 15 percent of the $303 million budget next year. But GEO has run the prison cheaper than the county ever could, Reilly said. And outsourcing still saves the government an estimated $3.2 million a year, according to Delaware County Executive Director Marianne Grace.

By having Reilly and his staff on the premises, the county's version of privatization is ideal because the government is able to keep an eye on GEO and implement hefty fines—more than $700,000 this year—when the jail is understaffed. "Our security, maintenance and food service is similar to, and in some instances maybe better, than when the county ran it," Reilly said.

Proponents of privatization say profit-driven companies can eliminate patronage jobs, play hardball with the labor unions and find new efficiencies without a substantial drop-off in services.

Prison privatization ... pits labor unions against politicians and corporate leaders against inmate-advocacy groups.

Government officials "tend to hire people that have worked on their campaigns or political-patronage people," Nunn said. "Corporations tend to hire people that are competent and capable. They can manage more effectively than a public entity can."

Critics say the profit incentive is a double-edged sword, and that the industry makes its money on the backs of inmates and guards by reducing personnel costs and cutting back on inmate care.

"I don't trust them as far as I can throw them," said Ken Kopczynski, executive director of the Private Corrections Institute and a lobbyist for the Florida Police Benevolent Association, a union that represents police and correctional officers. "All those millions of dollars they are making that are going into corporate executives' pockets should have been put into inmates services," he said.

Avalanche of Lawsuits

Delaware County officials say they are generally satisfied with GEO's performance here since 1996, with one large caveat: The medical services in the prison have, at times, fallen woefully short.

Employee turnover in that department has been extremely high in recent years, Reilly said, and the company has gone through eight health-services administrators since 2004. As a result, the daily "pill call" for inmates, for example, is sometimes run by nurses who are incompetent or overworked, he said, and the backlog of prisoners waiting for medical attention can exceed 400 cases. "The medical department has underperformed here," Reilly concedes.

Critics say the profit incentive is a double-edged sword, and that the industry makes its money on the backs of inmates and guards.

GEO has spent an inordinate amount of time and money fending off federal lawsuits, including wrongful-death cases. The frequent litigation is one of the main reasons the company is bailing out on its contract next week [December 2008].

In 2006, the company agreed to pay $100,000 to the family of Rosalyn Atkinson, a 25-year-old mother of two who died from a toxic dose of a blood-pressure drug while in prison custody. In October, GEO agreed to an undisclosed settlement in the case of Cassandra Morgan, 38, who died in 2006 of complications from an untreated thyroid condition while jailed on a shoplifting charge.

GEO also paid $125,000 in 2005 to the family of a prisoner who hung himself with his bootlaces and agreed to a $300,000 settlement in 2000 involving another suicide.

Fay Kallenbach and her attorney are awaiting more medical information before deciding whether to move forward with a lawsuit on behalf of her son, a longtime member of Howard Stern's "Wack Pack." Prison officials say they are not at fault in his death.

While the Delaware County prison was far from a utopia when it was run by the county—seven guards were convicted of federal charges stemming from inmate beatings in 1994—GEO's correctional officers have compiled a lengthy rap sheet since the jail was privatized.

This year a K-9 officer pleaded guilty to having sex with an inmate in his pickup truck, and a guard admitted to sending a forged letter to the state parole board so her boyfriend—a convicted murderer—could move in with her.

In 2006 the jail's former work-release supervisor, who is now registered under Megan's Law as a sex offender, pleaded guilty to sexually assaulting an inmate, and a guard pleaded guilty in federal court last year to conspiracy to commit bank robbery.

Two other guards were convicted of participating in a 2002 attack on an inmate who claimed that he was handcuffed and pummeled with a basketball and that his pants were pulled down. That inmate's attorney, Jon Auritt, has said the incident reminded him of "Abu Ghraib [a prison in Iraq], except without the dogs." GEO later paid an undisclosed settlement in that case, though.

Prison staff incorrectly released three inmates between 2002 and 2004, and in 2006, GEO agreed to pay a settlement to an innocent man who sued the company because he was imprisoned for more than 40 days. It was a case of mistaken identity.

GEO officials declined to be interviewed for this story, as did state Rep. John Perzel, R-Phila., a paid member of its board of directors. The company did not admit any wrongdoing in the lawsuits it settled.

Pennsylvania Counties Unreceptive

In 1998, the state Supreme Court approved the privatization of the Delaware County prison, ruling against the prison guards' union, which had filed suit to block the outsourcing. At the time, labor leaders fretted that the ruling would pave the way for other counties to hire firms to run their own jails. That never happened.

While privatization has taken off in other states, particularly Texas, the George W. Hill Correctional Facility remains the only privately run county prison in Pennsylvania, largely due to strong union resistance, according to Richard Culp, a prison privatization expert and professor at the John Jay College of Criminal Justice in New York City. "It's a matter of labor costs, pure and simple," said Culp, who has worked as a consultant for the Delaware County Board of Prison Inspectors.

Beaver County tried to privatize its prison in 2006, but was bombarded by union opposition. The county lost a ruling by an arbitrator, which was upheld in Common Pleas Court, according to county Commissioner Charles Camp. Beaver County officials decided not to appeal the case because the legal bills were getting so high, he said. "We had everyone coming at us," Camp said of the unions that fought the privatization proposal. "It would have saved us a million bucks a year," he said, adding that the county is now facing a $2 million budget deficit and is planning layoffs.

Large corrections companies increasingly are looking to the federal government for their profits, and U.S. Immigration and Customs Enforcement and other federal agencies have been expanding their use of private companies in recent years, Culp said.

While Culp recommended that counties and other government agencies keep a short leash on those firms—as Delaware County does—he said the industry has become more "professional" since the mid-1990s. "I think the market has shaken out a lot of the underperformers and poor performers and people that got into it to make a fast buck," Culp said.

Hope for the Future

Community Education Centers (CEC), a smaller, privately held company that specializes in inmate re-entry services, will replace the GEO Group on Jan. 1 [2009] at the Delaware County prison.

Based in West Caldwell, N.J., CEC operates county prisons in Texas, Arizona and Ohio, as well as treatment centers within publicly run prisons. In Philadelphia, it runs Hoffman Hall, a residential re-entry center for city inmates that opened in July, and Coleman Hall, which runs a work-release program for state inmates.

William Palatucci, a CEC senior vice president, said the Delaware County prison will become the largest county jail in the company's network. Most of the existing GEO guards will keep their jobs, and county officials say that guards that once worked for GEO are interested in coming back now that the company is leaving.

CEC made headlines in 2004 when a Coleman Hall resident was shot to death in his room, and the company is being sued by the Pennsylvania Institutional Law Project on behalf of several inmates who said they were denied adequate medical care there.

Palatucci declined to comment on the litigation, but said the company planned to bring to the Delaware County prison a "renewed commitment to quality operations." "I think competition is good for everybody. It keeps the public sector and private sector on their toes," he said. "At the end of the day, that's good for the taxpayer."

Robert Eskind, spokesman for the Philadelphia Prison System, said the city is "pleased so far" with CEC's performance at Hoffman Hall.

County officials say CEC could be a better fit than GEO at their jail, particularly because the company has experience in reducing recidivism. Overcrowding has long been a problem there.

John Hosier, chairman of the county Board of Prison Inspectors, is optimistic about the changing of the guard, but warned against unrealistic expectations. "We can hope for the best," Hosier said, "but it is a jail."

Some States May House Prisoners in Tents

Richard Luscombe

Richard Luscombe is a journalist whose articles have appeared in many newspapers worldwide.

Florida's balmy winter temperatures have long been a draw for visitors eager to spend some time under canvas, sleeping on cots and enjoying the great outdoors. But a new plan to expose some of the state's inmates to the delights of year-round 'camping' has failed to evoke the same enthusiasm.

Faced with a budget deficit of $2.3 billion, Florida is saving money by buying giant tents to house prisoners at nine of its 137 facilities. With its prison population having passed 100,000 for the first time this month [December 2008], corrections officials say that the hundreds of extra beds will also help address potential overcrowding problems.

The state isn't the first to try the idea. Michigan, Colorado, Arizona, and Hawaii are among those that have considered or used tents to better manage prison populations. But Florida, with the third-largest corrections system in the country (after California and Texas) is the biggest and the first to try it on such a scale.

So far 36 tents, each able to house 22 inmates, have been set up at eight prison sites in north Florida, and one in the south, and the state has 20 more in reserve.

Walter McNeil, secretary of the Florida Department of Corrections, insists that the move is temporary and that the tents are "a precautionary measure" that he hopes not to have to use.

Richard Luscombe, "At Overcrowded Florida Prisons, Some Inmates May Just Camp Out," *Christian Science Monitor*, December 30, 2008. Copyright © 2008 Christian Science Monitor. Reproduced by permission of the author.

Prisoner Advocates Skeptical

However, his claims cut little ice with prisoners' advocates, who say that the state has taken a stride backwards by erecting the structures and that Florida's notoriously high summer temperatures will make conditions intolerable for those housed within.

Michigan, Colorado, Arizona, and Hawaii are among those that have considered or used tents to better manage prison populations.

"However many they build, they're going to fill them," says Bill Sheppard, a Jacksonville attorney who has represented inmates in numerous actions involving prisoners' rights and conditions. "In August, in a tent, with the heat in Florida, your brain's going to boil, and that ain't a very good thing," Mr. Sheppard says. "They've tried this before, and were made to take the tents down, now they're trying it again and it will fail again."

"The technology of the type of tent may have changed, and the law may have changed, but it didn't work then and it won't work now," he says.

The US Supreme Court addressed the issue the last time that the Florida Department of Corrections used smaller tents to temporarily house inmates coming into the prison system before their assignment to a permanent facility. Although not specifically mentioned in the justices' decision at the time, the tents were among a number of measures adopted by Florida to tackle overcrowding that were ruled unconstitutional in the 1977 *Costello v. Wainwright* case.

Ironically, it was that action, finally settled in the middle of the last decade, which seems to have led indirectly to Florida looking again at canvas for convicts. With the intention of avoiding similar challenges from prisoners about conditions in overcrowded jails, state lawmakers mandated that its prison system must always carry a cushion of spare bed space.

Now, with an inmate population rising by more than 5 percent in 2007, faster than in any other state according to recently released figures from the Bureau of Justice Statistics, and the corrections department under pressure to trim its $2.3 billion annual spending, Florida has turned to the $9,000 tents.

Prisoners' advocates . . . say that the state has taken a stride backwards by erecting the structures and that Florida's notoriously high summer temperatures will make conditions intolerable.

This time, says corrections spokesperson Gretl Plessinger, the department looked at all the legal issues surrounding their use and was satisfied. "If our prison population spikes unexpectedly, or something happens such as a hurricane or other natural disaster, we might need to move our prisoners around quickly, and we have to have the capacity," says Ms. Plessinger. "In other states you have inmates sleeping on floors in corridors because of overcrowding, but by law that cannot happen in Florida," she says. "That's why we have the tents, as options only if we need them."

The department also has four permanent dormitories under construction, which will add several hundred more bed spaces to the prison system within the next few months. But even that might not be enough to prevent Florida moving inmates into the tents. "If the prison population keeps going up as projected, we will need the equivalent of 19 new prisons over the next five years," Plessinger says.

Florida's experiences with canvas will be watched closely by other states looking for a more permanent fix to their own problems in squaring growing prisoner numbers with shrinking budgets. In the past, tents have been favored elsewhere only as a short-term fix.

Arizona's Tough Example

One exception is in Maricopa County, Arizona, where hardline Sheriff Joe Arpaio set up a notorious city of heavy canvas prison tents 15 years ago. Like the new Florida tents, there is no air conditioning and inmates swelter in summer temperatures often in excess of 100 degrees F[ahrenheit].

"Is this a signal that we're also really getting tough [with our prisoners]?" says Professor Gordon Bazemore, chair of the department of criminal justice at Florida Atlantic University in Boca Raton. "I'm starting to wonder about the symbolism because I can't figure out why they're doing this, it makes no sense," he says. "I suspect they're trying to save money every way they can, which is true in every way in this state, but I also think there might be more to it than that."

Electronic Monitoring May Be an Effective Alternative to Prison

Dana DiFilippo

Dana DiFilippo is a reporter for the Philadelphia Daily News.

By the fall [2008], hundreds of convicted criminals could get sprung from Philadelphia's crowded jails and instead be under the "virtual lockdown" of a global positioning system [GPS].

But instead of a guardian angel crooning advice into their ears, a voice barking orders from their ankle—like a modern-day version of Maxwell Smart's shoe phone—would scold offenders who ventured someplace forbidden.

That's the vision of Deputy Mayor Everett Gillison, who plans to have a pilot program in place this fall [2008] in which more than 200 offenders would wear GPS-tracking anklets embedded with two-way speakers so that guards could immediately detect wayward wearers—and warn them to quit their wrongdoing or risk returning to jail.

The program would alleviate crowding in the city's jammed jails by removing nonviolent inmates, already sentenced for misdemeanors and "light felonies," and hooking them up to the GPS trackers, Gillison said.

Only one-fifth of the 9,300 inmates in city jails are there for violent offenses, a recent study found. About 37 percent of them already have been sentenced, prisons spokesman Robert Eskind said.

GPS monitoring also would save money, Gillison said. Inmates cost the city about $91 a day; Gillison estimates that GPS monitoring would cost $9 to $18 per day, per offender.

Dana DiFilippo, "City Eyes 'Virtual' Prisons to Help Clear Jammed Jails," *Philadelphia Daily News*, May 29, 2008. Copyright © 2008 Philly Online, LLC. All rights reserved. Reproduced by permission.

"You can't just lock people up and throw away the key; that mentality has pervaded our criminal-justice system for too long," said Gillison, who also is exploring alternatives like day-reporting, which would allow low-risk participants to be employed.

GPS Tracking

Gillison, Mayor Nutter's public-safety chief, has been meeting with companies offering the GPS technology and plans to put the plan out for bid soon. Not all companies include the speakers—which use cellular technology—with the GPS trackers.

About 800 offenders in Philadelphia already are electronically monitored, Court Administrator Dave Lawrence said. Under electronic monitoring, authorities know when offenders venture beyond defined areas.

The GPS technology allows authorities to know where offenders are at all times. That capability has some critics questioning whether the technology is too Orwellian [too much like the tactics of totalitarian governments as portrayed by the novelist George Orwell]. Others worry that offenders might become temporarily impossible to track if they pass through "dead zones" unreachable by the satellite technology.

District Attorney Lynne Abraham said yesterday that she hadn't seen Gillison's plan but that it needs "a lot of discussion." Such discussion, she said, should include making sure that a fair and adequate assessment is in place to determine who qualifies for GPS tracking and ensuring enforcement so that violators return to jail.

A prison also cannot overrule a court order, Abraham added, so Gillison's plan couldn't allow the release of inmates deemed serious offenders and sentenced to incarceration. "Public safety is our overarching concern," she said. "Nobody who's smoking a joint goes to prison. These people [jail inmates] are candidates who create certain concerns for public safety."

GPS [global positioning system] technology allows authorities to know where offenders are at all times.

Such concerns haven't stopped more than 350 jurisdictions nationwide from contracting with Utah-based SecureAlert, said Peter Derrick, a company spokesman.

In perhaps the device's most famous application, authorities last year used one to monitor the post-arrest movements of former astronaut Lisa Nowak, who was accused of driving across country and of donning a disguise in an ill-fated plot in February 2007 to kidnap and kill her perceived rival in a reported love triangle. The case remains unresolved. Derrick said SecureAlert is the only company offering the speaker technology.

It also frees up corrections personnel, because offenders' movements are tracked by SecureAlert staffers who notify local authorities if violations occur, Derrick said.

One prisoners' advocate applauded the technology as a positive alternative to incarceration. "There are a number of viable alternatives to locking somebody into a hard cell, and GPS is one," said Bill DiMascio, executive director of the Pennsylvania Prison Society. "We've been resistant to using some of these alternatives, for fear of being perceived as being soft on crime. But instead, they're a very smart way to deal with this growing and very costly problem [of crowded prisons]."

CHAPTER 4

How Are Recent Trends Affecting Prisons?

Chapter Preface

Prisons change from era to era. This chapter examines some of the recent trends, apart from increased overcrowding, that are challenging prison administrators and altering the prospects of inmates. Most of these trends have negative effects in terms of preparing prisoners to adapt to the outside world after release. But there are a few that offer hope to those who want to work toward self-improvement.

Ongoing searches of prisons, and of prisoners themselves, have become more intense recently. Inmates always have found ways to smuggle in forbidden items, but cell phones have heightened the serious effects of such contraband. Cell phones threaten security in and out of prisons, because they often are used by gang members to arrange crimes on the outside. For example, a Baltimore man was gunned down outside his home after a shooting suspect he identified ordered him killed from behind bars.

Another major problem nationwide is the advancing age of prisoners due to longer sentences and the fact that people are living longer. More and more inmates have age-related health problems, which puts great strain on prisons' medical facilities and increases the cost of prison operation. Whether elderly inmates who are unlikely to commit new crimes should be released is likely to become an increasingly important public debate in the future.

The issue of early release is a difficult one, and not only in overcrowded prisons. Many states have adopted "truth in sentencing" laws, which require convicts to serve their entire terms behind bars. In some prison systems parole is no longer a possibility. Yet without hope of parole, inmates have no incentive to educate themselves or perform constructive work. Many experts believe that it does no good to keep any but the most violent criminals in prison for life, because most crimes are committed by people under thirty, and those who made mistakes when young and impulsive are not apt to do so when they are older.

Most convicts who receive short sentences are sent to minimum-security prison camps, which once were known as comparatively pleasant places to serve time and were even dubbed "country clubs" by observers who considered them too soft. But now such camps are becoming more like regular prisons, with much more regimentation than they used to have. This is not only because of the trend toward getting tougher on crime, but because the white-collar criminals in such camps are now outnumbered by drug offenders.

The worst criminals, such as gang leaders, serial killers, and terrorists, are now frequently sent to so-called Supermax prisons, and inmates of regular prisons who habitually misbehave often are now sent there as well. In Supermaxes, prisoners are kept isolated in tiny concrete cells, are allowed out for only one hour a day, and have no contact with their fellow-inmates.

At the other end of the spectrum, there is a growing trend toward direct-supervision prisons, in which small groups of inmates interact with corrections officers in more normal surroundings than a traditional prison. Such prisons often have upholstered furniture, colorful walls, and carpet. Some criminologists believe if prisoners are treated as if good behavior is expected from them, they are more likely to comply than they would be under less humane conditions.

Although there is less effort today made toward rehabilitating prisoners than there was several decades ago, some rehabilitation programs do exist. One of the most notable examples is the growing use of inmates to train dogs, either to be good companion animals or as service animals for the blind and disabled. Often the prisoners transform themselves in the process of training the dogs.

Cell Phones Are a Growing Threat to Prison Security

Robert K. Gordon

Robert K. Gordon is a reporter for the Birmingham News.

A corrections officer making rounds last week in one of Elmore Correctional Center's open dormitories spotted an inmate in bed chatting away on a cell phone. If it had been a college dorm—no problem. But in prison, cell phones are off-limits. In a scene that corrections officials say is becoming increasingly familiar, the officer chased the inmate, caught him and took away the phone. Drugs and shanks are still around, but cell phones are the new contraband of choice in many federal and state prisons in Alabama and across the country. Inmates use the phones to continue conducting criminal enterprises or to stay in touch with family and friends, prison officials say.

But chatter causes problems in the lockup.

"It is a security concern. We have an agencywide prohibition against cell phones and we have security measures to prevent them from coming in," said Charles Sansum, spokesman at the Federal Correctional Institution at Talladega. "In a prison setting, we want to monitor the communication of inmates. It's hard to do that when they have cell phones."

Inmates and their friends on the outside are crafty when it comes to getting the phones behind bars. Sometimes people throw them over fences, smuggle them in shaving cream cans or even hide them in body cavities. And if the price is right, some prison staffers will risk bringing in phones to inmates, prison officials say.

Robert K. Gordon, "Battling Cell Phones in Alabama's Cellblocks," *Birmingham News*, February 22, 2009. Copyright © 2009 The Birmingham News. All rights reserved. Reprinted with permission.

Extent of the problem

State prison officials recently found about 60 cell phones, along with knives and other contraband, during a sweep of the state's oldest men's prison, 70-year-old Draper Correctional Facility in Elmore County.

"It's just exploding," said James DeLoach, the Alabama Department of Corrections associate commissioner. "Gangs are becoming more prevalent in our system now than they were five years ago. Gangs use cell phones to communicate with outside persons who relay information to inmates at other facilities. It's becoming very organized and it's statewide."

The problem is also nationwide, sometimes with deadly consequences.

In Maryland, an inmate used a mobile phone in 2007 to arrange the killing of a witness in a homicide case. A Maryland legislator got a phone call from a prisoner on a cell phone who called to complain about prison conditions. In Texas, a warden got a call from the mother of an inmate who wanted to know why her son's cell phone got such bad reception from behind bars.

Felicia Ponce, spokeswoman for the U.S. Bureau of Prisons in Washington, said the bureau doesn't keep statistics on the number of phones it confiscates. DeLoach said state prison officials seize hundreds of phones every year.

Inmates who have cell phones are violating prison rules, but because there is no law making it a crime for them to have the phones, their only punishment is a denial of prison privileges.

If finding the phones and preventing them from coming into a prison is hard enough, SIM cards make it that much harder, prison officials say. A phone won't work without a SIM—subscriber identity module—card. Several inmates who have memory chips can use a single phone simply by switching out the SIM card.

"We routinely train our staff on the detection of all contraband, including SlM cards, to ensure that inmates are not violating policy or engaging in unauthorized activities," Ponce said.

Smuggling them in

Inmates continue to find creative ways to get cell phones. Someone recently placed 10 phones in a mailbox at the home of an Alabama warden, DeLoach said. The plan was for an inmate garbage crew to come by and retrieve the package.

"Luckily the warden's children saw this strange car come up and put something in the mailbox and they alerted their dad," he said.

In prison, phones can cost as much as $300, especially for the more expensive models, such as a BlackBerry.

"It used to be we'd get the little cheap TracFones that you could get from Wal-Mart. Now we're getting BlackBerrys," said Capt. Richard Naile, a shift supervisor at Elmore Correctional Facility, one of two major prisons next to Draper. "Until they make it a crime for them to possess a cell phone, we're never going to stop it."

Last summer Naile said, members of the Correctional Emergency Response Team searched two of Elmore's three dorms, which are home to about 800 inmates. They found 80 cell phones. Thirteen more later were found in a pile of inmate clothing near the prison's back gate.

"So you're talking about some big money," said Vernon Barnett, the Alabama prison system's chief deputy commissioner. "It's not as if it were drugs where if you get caught bringing drugs into the prison, you're going to do some hard time. Cell phones are not illegal on the outside . . . so they're not risking quite as much."

Earlier this month, a shakedown at Donaldson Correctional Facility in west Jefferson County yielded 18 cell phones and three Bluetooth headsets. Also turned up were items that indicated traditional contraband is far from a thing of the past: 31 knives, a digital drug scale and packages of marijuana, cocaine and pills.

Many of the phones found in Alabama prisons—DeLoach figures about half—are brought in by staff members looking to make extra cash, officials said.

"We are prosecuting, of course," he said, "but district attorneys, with their caseloads being what they are, they're not placing a high priority on prosecuting a former correctional officer for smuggling cell phones."

Inmates who are caught with a phone can be punished through a loss of privileges, such as fewer visits to the prison store, or be given extra duties, Naile said.

Fighting the problem

Prisons across the country are trying to find ways to combat the problem, from high-tech sensors to dogs trained to sniff out cell phone parts. Mississippi is using metal detectors in Unit 32, its 1,000-bed maximum-security facility at the state penitentiary at Parchman, and spokesman Kent Crocker said the devices have helped reduce the number of illicit cell phone. Virginia uses dogs.

A prison in Texas recently experimented with jamming cell phone signals, but a demonstration of the jamming device was canceled after the state attorney told prison officials that jammers are illegal under federal law.

"Cell phones in prisons, as Yogi Berra would say, are ubiquitous and everywhere," said Terry Bittner, director of security products of ITT Corp., a Maryland-based company that works with prisons to keep cell phones out of inmates' hands.

Bittner said ITT has developed a system by which sensors are installed near cellblocks. If an inmate makes a call, receives a text message or simply turns on his phone, an alert is sent to a central server. The server locates the source of the signal.

A map of the facility flashes on a computer screen at a guard station, pinpointing the phone's location.

"It allows the staff to be much more efficient," Bittner said. "When doing a shakedown, they can target their search instead of looking in every cell."

Bittner said the technology has been used in several federal prisons since 2005. State prisons in Virginia, Pennsylvania and South Carolina also use it.

Alabama prison officials said that, for now, the system will depend on random shakedowns. "We've looked at various technology, but we haven't found anything yet that we'd be willing to open the pocketbook for," system spokesman Brian Corbett said.

In any event, the system would be hard pressed to find the dollars to buy the tools to combat cell phones. Corrections Commissioner Richard Allen said earlier this year that Alabama is 49th in the country in spending for prisoners, and Corbett said a single dog trained to detect mobile phones can cost as much as $25,000.

At Elmore, Warden Willie Thomas said part of the phone problem lies in the ratio of inmates to officers. During a typical shift at the prison, there are about 100 or more prisoners for each officer. The presence of more officers would reduce the cell phone flow, he said.

"It's simple arithmetic."

The Prison Population Is Aging

Carrie Abner

Carrie Abner is a senior policy analyst for Public Safety and Justice at the Council of State Governments.

At age 89, Earl takes six pills a day and carries a bottle of nitroglycerin pills with him at all times in case he has a heart attack or stroke. His fingers are shriveled with arthritis and he's had cataract surgery three times. He just received a wheelchair to help him get around.

From outside appearances, Earl may seem like most other elderly men in America with a growing list of age-related ailments. But while many of his peers reside in nursing homes and assisted living facilities, Earl will likely call Wisconsin's Oshkosh Correctional Institution home for the rest of his life.

Earl represents a growing number of elderly inmates in state prisons across the country. As this population continues to rise, states are taking note.

Elderly Inmates: A Growing Trend

According to the U.S. Justice Department's Bureau of Justice Statistics, the U.S. prison population has grown from just over 319,000 in 1980 to nearly 1.5 million in 2005.

Elderly inmates represent the fastest growing segment of federal and state prisons. A 2004 report by the National Institute of Corrections [NIC] states that the number of state and federal prisoners ages 50 and older rose 172.6 percent between 1992 and 2001, from nearly 42,000 to more than 113,000. Some estimates suggest that the elder prisoner population has grown by as much as 750 percent in the last two decades.

Carrie Abner, "Graying Prisons: States Face Challenges of an Aging Inmate Population," *State News*, November/December 2006, pp. 9–11. Copyright © 2006 The Council of State Governments. Reproduced with permission.

Experts say the growth of the elder inmate population is expected to continue. According to Jonathan Turley, a law professor at George Washington University and director of the Project for Older Prisoners, the population of prisoners ages 50 and older in the federal system grew from 11.3 percent of the total prison population in 1986 to 26 percent in 1989. He adds that even conservative estimates suggest that this population will represent 33 percent by 2010.

Why such a dramatic increase in the older prisoner population? Experts point to a number of reasons.

Elderly inmates represent the fastest growing segment of federal and state prisons.

First, the rise in older prisoners reflects the general aging of society. In 2003, there were an estimated 36 million individuals age 65 or older in the United States, comprising just over 12 percent of the total population. According to the Federal Interagency Forum on Aging-Related Statistics, the older population grew from 3 million to 35 million in the 20th century.

Officials also point to the get-tough-on-crime reforms of the 1980s and 1990s as contributing factors to the growing numbers of older prisoners. Mandatory minimum sentences, three-strikes rules and truth-in-sentencing laws established in recent decades are keeping more offenders in prison for longer periods of time. And inmates are living longer, meaning prisons continue to swell.

Tending the Elderly Behind Bars

For states, the challenges associated with an aging prisoner population are real and growing, yet statistics on the numbers of elderly inmates are difficult to project. This is due in part to variations in the definitions states have established for elderly prisoners. For instance, while Ohio defines elderly inmates as those aged 50 and older, Minnesota sets the age at 55. Michigan considers those 60 and above as elderly, while in Colorado, this designation is reserved for inmates 65 and older. Other states have no official age designation for the elderly prisoner population.

What's more, inmates tend to age faster than members of the general population. Research indicates that a prisoner's physiological age is, on average, seven to 10 years older than their chronological age. Therefore, a 50-year old inmate may likely experience the age-related health problems of a 60-year old on the outside.

A 50-year old inmate may likely experience the age-related health problems of a 60-year old on the outside.

Dr. David Thomas, who chairs the Department of Surgery at Nova Southeastern University and previously directed the Florida Department of Corrections' Office of Health Services, recalls one of his first encounters with older inmates. Having met a prisoner he thought to be 70 to 75 years old, he was surprised to learn that the inmate was just 54.

"Inmates appeared to be physically and medically older than their actual age," he said.

Thomas and others point to a number of factors contributing to this phenomenon, including lack of access to health care services prior to entry, poor dietary and exercise habits, and substance abuse.

A 2000 study by the Florida Department of Corrections' Office of Health Services found that almost two-thirds of inmates received their first significant health care experience, defined as any surgery or filled and started prescription, while in prison.

Stress also contributes to accelerated aging among inmates. "The stress of incarceration—including lack of support systems and a lack of trust in fellow inmates—leads to chronically stressful and debilitating environments," said Thomas.

As a result, older inmates tend to develop age-related health problems earlier. According to Turley, an elderly inmate will experience an average of three chronic illnesses during his or her term. The National Institute of Corrections lists arthritis, hypertension, ulcer disease, prostate problems and myocardial infarction among the most common chronic diseases among elderly inmates. Diabetes, Hepatitis C and cancer are also common.

The financial burden for states in providing adequate health care for older prisoners is staggering.

The financial burden for states in providing adequate health care for older prisoners is staggering. In 1997, the Texas Criminal Justice Policy Council reported that health care for elderly inmates ran $14.80 per day, nearly three times the health care costs for younger prisoners.

While a younger prisoner costs approximately $22,000 to house annually, states pay an average of $67,000 per year for older inmates.

And as the aging prisoner population grows, the costs for states are expected to rise. Experts estimated that annual costs for providing health care to elderly inmates in Texas could increase from $27 million in 1999 to $56 million in 2008.

Special Needs of Elderly Inmates

In addition to the rising health care costs, the aging prisoner population presents additional challenges for the states, including general accommodations and protection against younger offenders.

Like the elderly population outside prison walls, older inmates need special adaptive devices to help overcome physical impairments. For many elderly, walkers, canes, hearing aids, eyeglasses, dentures and geriatric chairs are necessary to function well.

Beyond meeting the general needs of an aging population, however, states must also address the specific needs of the aging population in prison settings. One of the primary challenges for states is adapting prison facilities that originally were not designed with elderly residents in mind.

"Prisons aren't geared to the needs and vulnerabilities of older people," said Brie Williams, MD, a geriatrician at the San Francisco VA Medical Center and lead author of a recent study on aging female prisoners. "In the prison environment, there are a number of unique physical tasks that must be performed every day in order to retain independence. They're not the same tasks that are called for in the community."

For some elderly prisoners . . . the general prison population can be threatening.

The study of 120 elderly female prisoners in California found that 69 percent reported that at least one activity of daily living was very difficult to perform. Sixteen percent reported that they needed assistance with at least one daily activity, representing twice the rate of the general U.S. population 65 or older.

In many cases, inmates rely on younger prisoners to get around.

For some elderly prisoners, however, the general prison population can be threatening. The NIC cites vulnerability of abuse and predation and difficulty in establishing social relationships with younger inmates as some of the specific challenges associated with an aging prisoner population.

According to a 2004 NIC report, "the lack of personal protection for elderly inmates, who may be frail and therefore vulnerable to the threats of assault by younger predatory inmates, contributes to the emotional stress and physical deterioration they routinely experience, especially among those who may be already vulnerable owing to chronic or terminal illness and who have few options for change in their environment."

States React: Programs and Policies for an Aging Prison Population

Across the country, states are beginning to take steps to address the implications of an older prison population. From developing targeted programs and activities for elderly inmates to providing specialized geriatric care, state corrections departments are devoting an increasing amount of attention and resources to the needs of seniors.

In a 2001 survey by the Criminal Justice Institute, approximately 15 of the 44 participating states and territories indicated that they provided supervised recreational programs specifically designed for older and elderly inmates. And other states have established educational programs on wellness and aging issues as part of an overall preventive care program.

Ohio's Hocking Correctional Facility offers a "50+ and Aging" program, which is designed to address the physical, psychological and social needs of older inmates. Such activities as chair aerobics, adult basic education and GED classes are provided as part of the program, as well as specialized recreational options, including bingo, shuffleboard, horseshoes and a walking program. Case managers also provide assistance to elderly inmates applying for Social Security and Medicare benefits.

Pennsylvania has also provided inmate health care education programs, and has even offered a healthy heart food line, featuring low fat, high fiber foods for inmates.

Specialized housing for elderly inmates appears to be another trend in the states. At least 16 states provide separate housing facilities for older prisoners; in seven states, these housing units are reserved for elderly inmates with special medical needs or for those otherwise eligible for hospice care.

The Minnesota Correctional Facility at Faribault, a medium-security facility for adult males, has a dedicated housing unit for inmates 55 and older with chronic health problems. Licensed practical nurses provide coverage 16 hours a day and around the clock nursing is offered in a clinic area.

Some states that do not have designated geriatric units have specified "chronic infirm" beds dedicated to older offenders. And approximately half the states offer hospice care for inmates.

At Angola State Penitentiary in Louisiana, once known as the bloodiest prison in America, death among inmates is now often due to natural causes. Facing a fast-growing population of elderly inmates, Angola is one of many prisons across the country that offers hospice care for inmates in the final stages of terminal illnesses. Fellow inmates build coffins and provide burial services for those who die inside.

Policymakers are considering whether some older inmates should be released through medical and early release programs.

A few states have even designated prisons for older inmates. Since 1996, Pennsylvania's State Correctional Institution at Laurel Highlands has been housing only elderly inmates and others who require long-term care or assisted living. Converted from a state mental hospital, the facility is designed to meet the needs of an older population, including long-term care inmates and wheelchair users.

Some officials argue that offering specialized facilities for older inmates and the chronically ill reduces the costs associated with their care, including medical, employment and transportation costs.

"Specialized camps provide economies of scale for the provision of targeted services," said Thomas. "Medical care, handicap facilities, specialized diets and specialized exercise regimens are all easier to provide when elderly inmates are in a single location."

He added that specialized facilities also experience fewer disciplinary problems, as older offenders are more protected from victimization by younger, more aggressive inmates.

Let Them Go?

Debate around the aging prison population has even extended beyond the prison walls. Across the country, corrections professionals, academics and policymakers are considering whether some older inmates should be released through medical and early release programs.

A number of states have compassionate release programs in place for terminally ill inmates, but some experts claim that these programs are rarely used, due to bureaucratic and other obstacles.

In Georgia, some elderly inmates have been released under medical reprieve, a supervised release program for inmates who are considered low-risk for re-offending. Proponents for this approach argue that once released, inmates may be eligible for Medicare, Social Security or veterans benefits, relieving a portion of the states' financial burden for their care.

Officials caution, however, that any cost savings from early release must be weighed against public safety risks and must consider the transfer of costs to other state programs.

"Although corrections may reduce costs through early release, the cost to taxpayers doesn't necessarily go away," said Carl Wicklund, executive director of the American Probation and Parole Association.

With little savings and limited employment opportunities, elderly offenders may not be able to adequately care for themselves. As a result, said Wicklund, "society may still be burdened by the costs for caring for an offender, even though he or she may no longer pose a threat to the community."

As America's prisoners continue to grow older and sicker, the costs to states will continue to rise.

Others agree, and advocate that some cost savings associated with early release programs be used to assist with the community re-entry transition. Testifying before the California Senate in 2003, Turley warned that "some of that money (from early release) has to be put back into the post-release plan. . . . It's not that expensive to do that. But it can be the difference between zero recidivism and greater recidivism. It's called a soft landing."

Looking Ahead

As America's prisoners continue to grow older and sicker, the costs to states will continue to rise. While states are beginning to address the needs of an increasingly aged prison population, experts warn that more planning must be undertaken to avoid a potential crisis down the road.

"States must prepare in the budgetary process to spend more on an aging inmate population," warned Thomas. He adds that funding requirements for the specialized diets and health care necessary for older prisoners must be considered.

Some officials also project that states may reconsider sentencing policies that keep offenders in prison for longer terms in an effort to curb prison growth.

As states try to find policy options for an ever-growing number of elderly inmates, prisoners like Earl continue to get older and sicker, requiring more care. To mitigate costs to taxpayers in the future, states should plan now.

Many States Have Eliminated Parole

Jens Soering

Jens Soering, who is serving a life sentence for crimes he insists he did not commit, is the author of several books on prison reform.

In 1981, at the age of 17, my friend Liam Q. did what many adventurous Kansas farm boys do: he joined the U.S. Navy to see the world. His test scores marked him for further training in a technical specialty, but Liam wanted to steer an aircraft carrier, so the navy made him a helmsman. Even today he gets excited when describing the delicate maneuvers required for a ship-to-ship resupply in rough seas.

As every sailor knows, shore leave is the most dangerous part of any cruise. This turned out to be true for Liam. At the naval base in Norfolk, Virginia, he fell in love with an older woman and was convicted of shooting her husband. In 1983, at the age of 19, he embarked on a different kind of cruise: a life sentence "up the river."

Liam was a typical murderer in two respects: he was young, and he knew his victim. Most homicides are committed not by strangers, but by young people who lash out at friends or family. These acts are often difficult to comprehend; they frequently are attributable to a confusing mixture of youthful angst, raging hormones, alcohol and drugs.

In those days, lifers entering the prison system were given a fairly standard orientation speech by their counselors. "Son, I know life seems hopeless right now," they were told, "but I am here to tell you that there is light at the end of the tunnel. If you keep your nose clean and don't break the rules—and if

Jens Soering, "Life without Parole," *Christian Century*, August 12, 2008. Copyright © 2008 by the Christian Century Foundation. All rights reserved. Reproduced by permission.

you do something to improve yourself while you're in here—then you can expect to leave this place one day. You're going to come up for parole for the first time 15 years from now, and of course you're not going to make it. But there's a good chance you'll make it on your third or fourth parole attempt, when you've served 18 or 19 years, if you can show the parole board that you've changed. So you can make it through this life sentence if you'll try."

That speech is no longer being given to fresh fish like Liam in many places today, because parole was abolished in a number of U.S. states during the 1990s and educational programs behind bars have been severely cut back.

Parole was abolished in a number of U.S. states during the 1990s and educational programs behind bars have been severely cut back.

The Parole System Rewarded Performance

But before we examine the shifting tides of correctional philosophy, let us spend a few moments to consider the old-fashioned, much-maligned, now vanishing parole system under which Liam began his sentence. What should strike us immediately is that it rewarded individuals for individual performance—the essence of applied conservative social theory. By contrast, consider the modern no-parole system, under which prisoners must serve a predetermined number of years—or, in the case of lifers like Liam, their entire lives—regardless of whether they better themselves or not. This is a case of one-size-fits-all bureaucratic thinking—individual differences, performance and initiative are sacrificed to the system.

Fortunately for Liam, parole still existed when he entered the Virginia Department of Corrections in 1983. Thus he began his life sentence with some version of the prison counselor's speech above, with light at the end of a very long tunnel.

At first, he ignored that distant hope completely. Prison affords a variety of opportunities to indulge despair, including every kind of drug imaginable, homebrewed alcohol, the tattoo subculture, situational homosexuality, gambling in its many forms, and the Dungeons & Dragons subculture. Liam fell prey to some of these dubious delights, as the Celtic tattoos on his biceps still attest. Since he could see no future, his present descended into near-total darkness.

[Elimination of parole] is a case of one-size-fits-all bureaucratic thinking—individual differences, performance and initiative are sacrificed to the system.

Then, some years into his sentence, Liam ran across *The Autobiography of Benjamin Franklin*—and his life changed. Across a 200-year divide, Ben Franklin, the archetypal American self-made man, persuaded a hopeless, young, life-sentenced convict that anyone could bootstrap his way out of misery. All it took was consistent hard work and the relentless pursuit of knowledge. Much like other inmates who read the Bible and find Jesus, Liam had discovered a good book and a savior. And Liam actually practiced what Franklin preached. One week at a time, Liam strove to acquire each of Franklin's 13 virtues, like thrift and prudence. Once he completed the list, he began anew, repeating the cycle four times annually. Liam followed this program for years.

The Importance of Lifelong Learning

A central feature of Franklin's philosophy was the importance of lifelong learning, whether the subject be new agricultural methods or the nature of electricity. While Liam did not go so far as to fly a kite in a thunderstorm, he did enroll in a four-year apprenticeship program as an electrician. His evenings were spent at community college classes, then still widely available and free of charge. After earning his degree, he studied Spanish, mathematics, physics and the real estate business through mail-order texts paid for by family members. Later he taught other prisoners these subjects at night—for a small gratuity, of course, since his mentor, Franklin, was also an astute entrepreneur. For fun and relaxation Liam learned how to crochet and cross stitch, on the principle that no skill is too humble for a true Renaissance man.

Around this time in the late 1980s, the first few computers began to filter into the correctional system. Prison administrators had little use for or interest in these strange new devices, but Liam was entranced by them. He ordered yet more textbooks through the mail and soon was in a position to explain to staff members how to operate their PCs. In the prison's maintenance department, where Liam had been working as a fully qualified electrician, the civilian supervisors made him their on-site information technology specialist, and he streamlined and computerized all processes from the ordering of spare parts to the scheduling of work orders. Word spread, and soon security staff started coming to him for help, too.

In the penitentiary, guards usually reward inmates for such extraordinary services with packs of cigarettes, bags of sugar (to brew "mash"), hardcore pornography or even drugs. The only payment Liam wants is more time on the computer, so he can keep on refining his skills.

Because Liam became particularly adept at desktop publishing, a reform-minded warden asked him a few years ago to manage and edit a quarterly newsletter for the inmate population. Liam turned this into his version of *Poor Richard's Almanack*, a compendium of practical advice ("how to avoid athlete's foot in penitentiary showers") and editorials on the power of positive thinking ("it's all about the choices we make"). The newsletter's banner would have made Ben Franklin proud: "To Encourage—To Inform—To Educate—To Inspire."

But for the past two years, Liam's energy for bootstrapping has been lagging. His newsletters appear less frequently. When I asked him recently to write down some aphorisms of Franklin's, he chose this one: "He that lives upon hope will die fasting." Having followed Franklin's gospel of perpetual self-improvement for more than two decades, Liam is discovering that there are some holes so deep that no amount of self-improvement can lift you out.

Parole abolition, also known as "truth in sentencing," is a criminal-justice fad that swept the nation in the mid-1990s.

The promise Liam's prison counselor made in 1983—that he could expect to be paroled after 19 years if he could demonstrate change—was broken in 2002. At this writing [2008], Liam is in the 25th year of his incarceration, and there is no realistic prospect of release—ever. So he is slowly slipping back into the state of complete despair in which he began his life sentence.

Life Sentences Now Truly Mean Life

What has brought Franklin's most faithful disciple so low? Parole abolition, also known as "truth in sentencing," is a criminal-justice fad that swept the nation in the mid-1990s. Forty states enacted truth-in-sentencing statutes, which require felons to serve as much as a full 85 percent of their prison terms without any chance of parole; life sentences now truly mean life. At the time this sounded like a good, conservative, law-and-order response to crime. The Violent Crime Control and Law Enforcement Act of 1994 offered prison construction grants and other financial incentives to states that passed truth-in-sentencing bills. Virginia's Republican governor (and later U.S. senator) George Allen was among the first to take the bait, abolishing parole in 1995. Now, the Virginia Department of Criminal Justice Services reports, "a large number of violent offenders are serving two, three or four times longer under truth-in-sentencing than criminals who committed similar offenses under the parole system."

The United States has created something never before seen in its history and unheard of around the globe: a booming population of prisoners whose only way out of prison is likely to be inside a coffin.

The no-parole policy technically applies only to those offenders sentenced after the passage of the truth-in-sentencing statute. For a so-called old-law prisoner like Liam, the possibility of parole still exists in theory. But the Virginia parole board and its counterparts across America took careful note of the signs of the times—board members are political appointees—and dramatically cut back the number of discretionary discharges. In Virginia, for instance, the parole grant rate for all eligible male convicts typically ranges around 2.9 percent. The figure for lifers is close to 0 percent.

By virtually eliminating parole even for those life-sentenced inmates who are technically still eligible, Virginia is merely following a strong nationwide trend. The Sentencing Project reports that U.S. penitentiaries held 127,677 lifers in 2004, of whom only a few dozen are paroled each year. In California, with the nation's largest prison system, a federal district court found in 2005 that the parole board "operated under a sub rosa policy that all murderers [typically serving life terms] be found unsuitable for parole." According to the *New York Times*, "The United States has created something never before seen in its history and unheard of around the globe: a booming population of prisoners whose only way out of prison is likely to be inside a coffin."

The Bureau of Justice Statistics has determined that lifers released prior to 1995 have the lowest recidivism rate of any group of offenders—less than one-third the rate of property or drug offenders, for instance.

One simple but important reason that lifers on parole pose such a low risk is their age: even before truth-in-sentencing, virtually no lifers were released until they reached their late 30s. By that time, they had aged out of their crime-prone years, explains Virginia's attorney general Robert F. Mc-Donnell: "Most serious crimes are committed by people between the ages of 18 and 32."

Parole Abolition Is a Goldmine for the Prison Industry

If abolishing parole for lifers does not make America's streets appreciably safer, what can explain the continuing popularity of this policy? That question has many answers: a punitive (as opposed to restorative) concept of justice, fear of crime, ignorance of criminological statistics, unfamiliarity with actual lifers like Liam, displaced aggression and frustration, and so on. What is often overlooked, however, is the role of money.

[Private prison operators] see jail and prison budgets as a recession-proof goldmine.

When the truth-in-sentencing concept was invented in the early 1990s by the American Legislative Exchange Council, it received massive federal support, making parole abolition its most successful legislative venture ever. On the committee that created the model statute sat representatives of the Corrections Corporation of America (CCA), one of the leading private prison operators in the nation.

Taxpayers see the $63 billion-a-year correctional system as another expensive government bureaucracy; each convict is an additional financial burden. Companies like CCA, on the other hand, see jail and prison budgets as a recession-proof goldmine; every inmate is worth $22,650, the annual per capita cost of incarceration. With 2.3 million convicts in the U.S., the money-making opportunities are extraordinary.

By 2025, one in four inmates will be elderly—a bonanza for the prison industry.

Beyond the CCA, the economic boon goes farther. Building the physical infrastructure to house this population affords $4.3 billion annually. Feeding convicts is the key to Aramark Correctional Services' success. The world's third-largest food services company provides a million meals a day to inmates in 1,500 private and government-operated facilities. Managing prison infirmaries is a business worth $2 billion per annum to Correctional Medical Services and Prison Health Services. Providing telephone services to convicts earns AT&T, Verizon, Sprint and others $1 billion a year. Putting inmates to work in factories and call centers behind walls generates another $1.5 billion worth of goods and services annually.

The financial incentive to keep lifers like Liam in prison is especially great. These men and women inevitably develop age-related medical problems as they grow old, raising their annual per capita cost of incarceration to $69,000. Once again, taxpayers may see this as bad news, but companies see a $69,000-a-year inmate as a cash cow.

Consider all the special, additional requirements of elderly convicts: wheel-chair accessible dormitories, hip replacement surgery, low sodium and diabetic diets, etc. Is it any wonder that prisoners aged 55 and over are one of the fastest growing demographic groups in the correctional population? By 2025, one in four inmates will be elderly—a bonanza for the prison industry. Already 35 states have built so-called geriatric prisons, and 29 have even set up end-of-life units. In all likelihood, that is where Liam will die a few decades from now.

Older Prisoners Who Committed Crimes in Their Teens Should Be Released

Ironically enough, the best hope of help that inmates like Liam may have comes from someone who once worked hard to enact truth-in-sentencing: Mark L. Earley, the former Republican attorney general of Virginia and current president of Prison Fellowship Ministries (PFM). During his ten years as state senator and four as attorney general, Earley spent most of his time "working on how to put more people in jail and keeping them there longer," he said in a speech at the Washington Convention Center. "I really pretty much had the view that prisoners were at the end of the line—that if you were in prison, you had no hope, you'd made a mess of your life, and it was better for me that you were there, because my family could be safe."

But Earley's attitude changed when he joined PFM following his 2001 defeat in Virginia's gubernatorial election. Riding his Harley-Davidson motorcycle from penitentiary to penitentiary to hold worship services, he met some of the men and women affected by truth-in-sentencing and similar policies. "I've seen an awful lot of prisoners that committed crimes in their late teens, early 20s," Earley told the *Virginia-Pilot*. "What happened was a terrible act of misguided youth. . . . Now they're in their 40s or 50s and they shouldn't be in prison any more." Earley gives newspaper interviews and appears on public television to lobby for change. "After a significant period of the sentence is served," he asks, "should we provide some opportunity for a look back?"

Prison Camps Can No Longer Be Dismissed as "Country Clubs"

Luke Mullins

Luke Mullins is an associate editor at U.S. News, *covering banking, real estate, and white-collar crime.*

Alfred A. Porro Jr. came to Allenwood in a large transport bus guarded by a handful of armed corrections officers. Like the five other prisoners on board, he arrived in full shackles. As the bus rumbled to a stop, the officers escorted the new inmates off the vehicle and turned them over to their keepers.

Porro disembarked with relief. Over the past two days, he had been whisked from one prison to another—no one would tell him where he was headed. Now, at least, Porro knew he would be serving his time at a minimum-security prison camp. Good news, he thought. And the grounds, Porro had to admit, were less than intimidating. With sweeping grasslands and thickets of trees, the camp presented none of the chilling images that the term "prison" calls to mind. No fences, no coiled razor wire, no sharpshooters on towers. It might as well have been a college campus. . . .

Welcome to Prison Camp

Like many other white-collar convicts, Porro wound up in a prison camp—a punishment often dismissed as a Club Fed holiday for wealthy, well-connected criminals, who spend their days sunbathing and working on their short irons. But scores of interviews with former inmates, legal experts, academics, members of advocacy groups, and others who know prisons

Luke Mullins, "Enter a 'Hellish Place,'" *American: A Magazine of Ideas*, May/June 2007. Copyright © 2007 American Enterprise Institute for Public Policy Research. Reproduced with permission of The American Enterprise, a national magazine of Politics, Business, and Culture (TAEmag.com).

paint a starkly different picture. In recent years, changing demographics, tighter regulations, and lengthening sentences have combined to make life in prison camps more and more similar to life in higher-security facilities. "It's not Yale, it's jail," says Dennis Faulk, a retired employee of the Federal Bureau of Prisons who spent part of his 27-year career at Allenwood prison camp. "We don't separate a white-collar guy from an organized-crime guy from a bank robber—they're all the same."

Certainly, if you have to go to jail, federal prison camp is the place to be. But for inmates who have left behind powerful jobs, close families, and abundant lifestyles, prison camp can present significant hardships. "You've been giving orders your whole life, and now there's this buffoon with an IQ of 20 telling you to clean the toilet—and you've got to do it," said one representative of a prisoner-advocacy group.

After serving five years in two different facilities, Porro reflected on his experience. "It's a hellish place," he said, "especially for a white-collar guy."

In recent years, changing demographics, tighter regulations, and lengthening sentences have combined to make life in prison camps more and more similar to life in higher-security facilities.

'You're Alone'

The Allenwood Federal Correctional Complex is tucked into the foothills of the northern Allegheny Mountains, 11 miles south of Williamsport, Pennsylvania, where the Little League World Series is held each year. In 1999, the complex—which sprawls over 640 acres of delightful countryside, smack in the middle of the state—comprised four different facilities: a high-security penitentiary, a medium-security correctional institution, a low-security correctional institution, and a minimum-security camp. A mile-long stretch of road, twisting through thinning woodlands, separates the camp from the other three facilities. From Porro's vantage point, as he disembarked from the van in the camp parking lot, he couldn't see the grim buildings that confine some of America's worst villains.

Instead, he faced a cement staircase leading up to a network of squat, red-brick buildings, where less violent convicts do their time. Alongside the housing units and administration buildings are such amenities as a gym, a softball diamond, a bocce pitch, and a tennis court slipped inside an oval track. From the grounds, inmates gaze at the soft mountaintops that rim the horizon. Deer poke their heads out of tall brush and dart into the forest, as groups of wild turkey gobble across the grass. . . .

Instead of cells, Allenwood camp inmates lived in cubicles, which were arranged in three rows covering the length of the room. The setup felt more like an army barracks than a prison. Just like all the others, Porro's cubicle was a tight fit for two people—nothing but a bunk bed and a split-level locker on a plain linoleum floor. After showing Porro to his new home, the officers quickly departed. "It's like being dropped in a strange country," Porro said. "Although there's a lot of people around, you're alone." . . .

Multiculturalism

To Porro, the biggest initial surprise about life at Allenwood was the diversity of his fellow inmates. Most of the camp prisoners were not the rich white guys he had expected to see, but poor African Americans and Hispanics—most of whom, Porro would soon learn, were drug offenders. "I was of the impression that the camps were primarily for white-collar criminals," Porro said. "That's just not the case."

Despite widespread perceptions to the contrary, minimum-security prison camps are not reserved for former congressmen and CEOs. "People assume that you go to a prison surrounded by lawyers, doctors, and politicians," said David Novak, a former inmate who is now president of a consulting firm that prepares convicts for prison life. "In fact, when you go to a camp, a full 70 percent of the other inmates are there as a direct result of the war on drugs." In 1970, according to the *Sourcebook of Criminal Justice Statistics*, drug offenders made up just 16 percent of all federal prisoners, but by January 2007, the proportion had risen to 54 percent.

Older inmates . . . often found it difficult to complete the daily chores that camp life demanded.

In part because of the increasing number of drug convictions, the federal prison system has expanded on a massive scale—from just 21,000 inmates in 1970 to 193,000 in 2007. As the system struggled to accommodate the ballooning population, many nonviolent drug offenders were sent to the camps. As a result, when new inmates like Porro arrive, they enter an unlikely community where the nation's elite—professionals, politicians, corporate executives—live alongside the indigent foot soldiers of the drug trade. . . .

'Watch Your Backside'

Older inmates like Porro often found it difficult to complete the daily chores that camp life demanded. For help, they turned to a group of inmates that he called "odd-jobs guys." In exchange for fees, such inmates would clean your room, do your laundry, or take care of any other small-scale inconvenience. Since currency is not permitted on the grounds, inmates barter. For example, an odd-jobs guy might wash Porro's clothes in return for, say, a pack of cigarettes. At Allenwood, the odd-jobs guys were generally drug offenders, Porro said, but certain white-collar inmates, particularly those that had been cleaned out by the feds, would also offer their services. . . .

Because minimum-security federal prison camps are generally limited to offenders who have not committed violent crimes, inmates are unlikely to encounter prison riots, forced sodomy, or the other terrifying hallmarks of higher-security institutions. But camp inmates also can't afford to relax. After all, most of their peers are gutsy streetwise men from hardscrabble backgrounds; these inmates may not have been convicted of violent crimes, but that doesn't mean they don't have a violent past

"Even though they weren't hardened criminals, you had to watch your backside," said David London, a former bank CEO who served time at a federal prison camp after he was convicted of embezzling more than $400,000. Violent incidents at federal prison camps tend to occur during downtime. "One of the things I learned quickly is you don't play basketball," said Webster Hubbell, associate U.S. attorney general—the third-highest Justice Department official—under President Clinton. Hubbell spent 18 months at a federal prison camp after pleading guilty to mail fraud and tax evasion.

"Most of the fights in prison that I witnessed emanated from the TV," said Nicholas Wallace, the former president of ESM Government Securities, Inc., who spent six years at two federal prison camps after his $350 million fraud drove 69 Ohio S&Ls [savings and loan banks] into bankruptcy. Wallace recalled a group of imposing drug offenders who used intimidation to control the television room of a Florida prison camp. In one particularly disturbing incident, Wallace witnessed an inmate being thrown through a glass window after a disagreement regarding which TV program to watch. "They lost their tempers, and one of them came flying through the window," Wallace said. . . .

One reason violence in prison camps remains low is that authorities impose harsh punishment on anyone involved.

Prisoners who get in a fight are immediately removed from the camp and reassigned to a higher-level facility. It's a powerful threat.

Boring Routine

Porro quickly learned to move to the drumbeat of prison life. Lights on at 5:00 a.m., down to the cafeteria by 6:00 a.m., clean up your cubicle before reporting to work by 7:00 a.m., break for lunch at 11:30 a.m., back to work at 1:00 p.m., and knock off at 3:30 p.m. Dinner is at 5:00 p.m. and mail call shortly thereafter. Lights out at 10:00 p.m. Meanwhile, corrections officers counted the inmates throughout the day to ensure that no one had escaped.

Porro's first job was in the kitchen, where he spent seven hours a day wrapping silverware into napkins for about $8 a week. Other inmates had jobs mopping floors, cleaning bathrooms, or landscaping the grounds of Allenwood's higher-security facilities—a detail that was considered favorable because it allowed them to work outdoors.

Boredom . . . can be a powerful enemy, especially for white-collar inmates who once held positions of tremendous power and responsibility.

When inmates finished work in the early afternoon, the rest of the day was theirs. Some lifted weights, ran laps, and participated in intramural sports. Although not particularly appetizing, prison meals were generally healthy. Alcohol and drugs, of course, were strictly prohibited. "I have heard a lot of people say that the two to four years I spent in jail probably added ten years to my life," Morze said. "You got in the best shape of your life, and there were no toxins."

Boredom, meanwhile, can be a powerful enemy, especially for white-collar inmates who once held positions of tremendous power and responsibility. "Your life is a big blah," Porro said. "I went from moment-to-moment busyness to basically doing nothing." To keep their minds active, some inmates become voracious readers; others embrace religion or take up new hobbies, like leatherwork. But Porro soon found a different distraction. As inmates learned he was a lawyer, they began asking Porro for his help writing legal briefs or appeals. . . .

A Harsher Prison Life

Life in federal prison camps has grown less comfortable for inmates over the years. When Morze was incarcerated in Lompoc, corrections officers and administrators would wistfully recall the good old days of the 1970s, when several Watergate conspirators were imprisoned there. Back then, inmates would order expensive chili from the legendary Chasen's restaurant in Beverly Hills, or maybe shoot a few holes of golf at a neighboring course. Occasionally, an inmate would even sneak out for a late-night visit to the prostitutes who were huddled in the back of a Winnebago parked nearby, the prison officials told Morze.

But new restrictions eliminated such flagrant disparities between prison camps and higher-security facilities, said Novak, the former inmate who is now a consultant. In years past, camp inmates could receive work assignments in nearby communities, allowing them to get off the prison grounds on a regular basis. They enjoyed a liberal furlough policy, enabling them to spend entire weekends away from the camp. Inmates could wear their own clothes while they did their time. There was no spending limit at the commissary or time limit on telephone use.

But all that has changed. Today, nearly all inmates remain on the grounds for their entire sentences, wearing prison-issued uniforms just like inmates at higher-security facilities. Each month, inmates can spend no more than $290 at the commissary and 300 minutes on the telephone. At the same time, regulations regarding camp visits have tightened, and inmates seeking to complete their sentences at halfway houses face more hurdles.

Taken together, the measures have created a surprising degree of parity between the camps and other prisons. "All the regulations are the same. They don't change just because you're at a camp," said Bryan Lowry, president of the Council of Prison Locals, a union representing federal corrections officers. "The Bureau of Prisons is the Bureau of Prisons." The changes were an effort to fight the perception that prison camps are unduly cushy, Novak said. "The Bureau of Prisons is incredibly sensitive to accusations that they are coddling white-collar offenders," Novak said. "They are very sensitive to the 'Club Fed' mythology." . . .

Recently convicted CEOs are now receiving sentences that had previously been reserved for perpetrators of violent crimes like rape and murder.

The Terms Grow Longer

"The high-profile scandals have generated more public concern about white-collar crime, and I think judges are no doubt aware of that," said Marc Mauer, the executive director of The Sentencing Project, a Washington, D.C.-based organization that supports reform of the criminal justice system.

As a result, recently convicted CEOs are now receiving sentences that had previously been reserved for perpetrators of violent crimes like rape and murder. . . . And these executives aren't sent to prison camps, which are limited to inmates with less than ten years to serve. Instead, they must serve their long sentences in higher-security facilities with some of the most violent criminals in America.

In the face of this trend, a small cadre of academics and advocacy groups has begun to argue that the government has gone too far in its punishment of white-collar criminals. "These draconian sentences have reached astronomic proportions," [Ellen S.] Podgor [associate dean and professor at Stetson University College of Law] said. Julie Stewart, the president of Families Against Mandatory Minimums, an organization working to reform sentencing laws, agreed. "I think the white-collar offenders are, by and large, getting more than they deserve," she said.

But as the widening gap between high- and low-income Americans becomes a focus for politicians and journalists, such arguments are unlikely to find much support. "People say, 'Listen, you had it all, and you messed up, so why should we have sympathy for you when some kid who was dealing crack didn't have any of these chances?'" Shapiro said.

"What people don't understand is that all people—rich or poor—have demons." . . .

More Prisoners, Less Crime

The striking growth of the federal prison population was triggered by a change in the American philosophy of criminal justice that occurred in the early 1970s, says Douglas A. Berman of the Moritz College of Law at Ohio State University. Berman, an expert on criminal law and sentencing, said that before that time, Americans had taken a European approach to incarceration, viewing prisons as places to rehabilitate criminals and return them to society as healthy, productive citizens. But this "enlightened" model fell out of favor. "Crime rates were rising throughout the 1950s and 1960s," Berman said. "People on both the right and the left concluded that we were doing more harm than good in the name of rehabilitation."

Since then, the prison system has evolved into a method for punishing lawbreakers and keeping them off the street. As the new approach—predicated on the idea that more prisoners equal less crime—became more popular, the inmate population marched upward, Berman said. In 1985, there were roughly 744,000 men and women in custody at federal, state, and local prison facilities. But by June 30, 2005, that figure had grown to nearly 2.2 million, according to the *Sourcebook of Criminal Justice Statistics*.

The get-tough approach pleased the public in other ways. The increase in prison facilities for the expanding inmate population created steady jobs and stimulated economic activity. Meanwhile, media reports of former inmates committing violent crimes after release hardened attitudes toward prisoners, Berman said. The trend has affected criminals of all stripes: the drug addict who robs a convenience store, the jealous husband who kills his wife's lover, the stockbroker who steals from his clients, and the CEO who cooks the books.

More Criminals Are Being Sent to Supermax Prisons

Jeffrey Ian Ross

Jeffrey Ian Ross is an associate professor in the Division of Criminology, Criminal Justice and Forensic Studies at the University of Baltimore.

Each time a crime occurs, an arrest is made, the trial ends, and a person is sentenced to prison, the public has a recurring curiosity about where the convict is sent. Over the past two decades, a phenomenal number of individuals have been sentenced to jails and to state or federal prisons.

But this is just the beginning of the journey. Prisoners are classified into a whole host of various kinds of facilities. They typically vary based on the level of security, from minimum to high. But since the mid-1980s, a dramatic change has underscored corrections in the United States and elsewhere. Correctional systems at all levels have introduced or expanded the use of Supermax prisons.

Supermax prisons, also known as Administrative Control Units, Special (or Security) Handling Units (SHU), or Control Handling Units (CHU) (Here, "CHUs" is pronounced "shoes.") are stand-alone correctional facilities, wings or annexes inside an already existing prison. They are a result of the recent growth in incarceration that has occurred throughout many of the world's advanced industrialized countries.

There is, however, a well-documented turning point in the history of Supermax prisons. In October 1983, after the brutal and fatal stabbings of two correctional officers by inmates at the federal maximum-security prison in Marion, Illinois, the

Jeffrey Ian Ross, "Supermax Prisons," *Society*, March/April 2007, pp. 60–64. Copyright © 2007 Springer Science & Business Media. Reproduced with kind permission from Springer Science & Business Media, conveyed through Copyright Clearance Center, Inc., and the author.

facility implemented a 23-hour-a-day lockdown of all convicts. The institution slowly changed its policies and practices and was retrofitted to become what is now considered a Supermax prison. Then, in 1994, the federal government opened its first Supermax prison in Florence, Colorado, specifically designed to house Supermax prisoners. The facility was dubbed the "Alcatraz of the Rockies."

Research on Supermax Prisons

Although much has been written on jails, prisons, and corrections, the mass media and academic community have been relatively silent with respect to Supermax prisons—and with good reason. It is difficult for journalists and scholars to gain access to prisoners, correctional officers, and administrators inside this type of facility. Reporting on correctional institutions has never been easy, and many editors and reporters shy away from this subject matter. Correctional professionals are also reluctant to talk with outsiders for fear that they may be unnecessarily subjected to public scrutiny....

As a response to an increased public fear of crime and to the demise of the "rehabilitative ideal," a punitive agenda took hold of criminal justice.

There are many unanswered questions about Supermax prisons. Why are Supermax prisons necessary? What particular circumstances led to the creation of Supermax prisons in different states and countries? Is the construction and increased reliance on Supermax institutions due to the fact that today's prisoners are more incorrigible and dangerous, and thus more difficult to handle? Or is it a reflection of the correctional system's failure or mismanagement, or pressures by the general public for a get-tough stance against dangerous criminals? Who are the typical persons sent to Supermax prisons? Why have the Supermax prisons and similar institutions in other countries engendered intense public outcry? What are the similarities and differences among American supermaxes and comparable facilities elsewhere?

Why Supermaxes Have Proliferated

Since the mid-1980s, many state departments of corrections have built their own Supermax prisons. Several reasons can account for their proliferation. First, many states had similar experiences to the blood that spilled at Marion. In Minnesota, for example, the escape of a prisoner, kidnapping of correctional officers, fatal stabbing of a warden, and a series of prison disturbances in the early 1970s created an environment that was ripe for the construction of a new facility that would house the "worst of the worst." Another explanation for the growth of Supermax prisons lies in the development of a conservative political ideology that began during the Reagan administration (1981–1989). As a response to an increased public fear of crime and to the demise of the "rehabilitative ideal," a punitive agenda took hold of criminal justice and led to a much larger number of people being incarcerated.

Reagan's Republican successor, George H.W. Bush, continued this approach from 1989 to 1993. Since then several factors prompted a dramatic increase in the number of people entering jails and prisons: the construction of new correctional facilities; new and harsher sentencing guidelines (particularly "truth in sentencing" legislation, mandatory minimums, and determinant sentencing); the passage of "three strikes you're out" laws and the war on drugs.

Another factor that contributed to the growth of Supermaxes is the careerism of correctional administrators.

In short, many of the gains that were part of the so-called "community corrections era" of the 1960s were scaled back. Congress and state legislatures passed draconian laws that reversed such time-honored practices as indeterminate sentencing and invoked a host of laws that lengthened prison sentences for convicted criminals.

Supermaxes are increasingly used for persistent rule-breakers, convicted leaders of criminal organizations (e.g., the mafia) and gangs, serial killers, and political criminals (e.g., spies and terrorists).

Another factor that contributed to the growth of Supermaxes is the careerism of correctional administrators. Some have argued that without the leadership of particular wardens, government rainmakers, and commissioners and/or secretaries of respective state Departments of Corrections, Supermax facilities would never have been built in the first place. Finally, it should be understood that, in many respects, Supermaxes symbolize the failure of rehabilitation and the inability of policymakers and legislators to think and act creatively regarding incarceration. Supermax prisons are excellent examples of the way that America, compared to other countries, has dealt with lawbreakers.

Originally designed to house the most violent, hardened, and escape-prone criminals, Supermaxes are increasingly used for persistent rule-breakers, convicted leaders of criminal organizations (e.g., the mafia) and gangs, serial killers, and political criminals (e.g., spies and terrorists). In some states, the criteria for admission into a Supermax facility and the review of prisoners' time inside (i.e., classification) are very loose or even nonexistent. These facilities are known for their strict lockdown policies, lack of amenities, and prisoner isolation techniques. Escapes from Supermaxes are so rare that they are statistically inconsequential.

In the United States alone, 6.47 million people are under the control of the criminal justice system. Approximately 2.3 million are behind bars in jails or prisons, while 3.8 million are on probation and 725,527 are on parole. The Supermaxes, maintained by the Federal Bureau of Prisons (FBOP) in Marion and Florence, for example, incarcerate 1,710 people—including such notable political criminals as "Unabomber" Ted Kaczynski and Oklahoma City bombing co-conspirator Terry Nichols.

Nevertheless, only a fraction of those incarcerated in state and federal prisons are sent to a Supermax facility. In 1998, approximately 20,000 inmates were locked up in this type of prison, representing less than 2 percent of all the men and women currently incarcerated across the country. Most of the U.S. Supermaxes, such as the federal facility in Florence, are either brand new or nearly so; others, however, are simply free-standing prisons that have been retrofitted. Meanwhile, the number of convicts being sent to Supermax prisons is steadily growing.

Many prisons have earned their individual reputations largely through well-known events that have taken place within their walls and have subsequently been covered by the media. Places like Attica, Folsom, San Quentin, Sing Sing, and Stateville are etched in the consciousness of many Americans. The Supermaxes, on the other hand, are known for their conditions and effects on prisoners within their walls.

[Supermaxes] are known for their strict lockdown policies, lack of amenities, and prisoner isolation techniques.

Conditions of Confinement

Although cells vary in size and construction, they are generally built to the dimensions of 12 by 7 feet. A cell light usually remains on all night long, and furnishings consist of a bed, a desk, and a stool made out of poured concrete, as well as a stainless steel sink and toilet.

One of the more notable features of all Supermax prisons is the fact that prisoners are usually locked down 23 out of 24 hours a day. The hour outside of the prison is typically used for recreation or bathing/showering. Other than their interaction with the supervising correctional officers (COs), prisoners have virtually no contact with other people (either fellow convicts or visitors). Access to phones and mail is strictly and closely supervised, or even restricted. Reading materials are often prohibited. Supermax prisoners have very limited access to privileges such as watching television or listening to the radio.

There is absolutely no personal privacy; everything the convicts do is monitored, usually through a video camera that is on all day and night.

Supermax prisons also generally do not allow inmates either to work or congregate during the day. In addition, there is absolutely no personal privacy; everything the convicts do is monitored, usually through a video camera that is on all day and night. Any communication with the correctional officers most often takes place through a narrow window on the steel door of the cell, and/or via an intercom system.

In Supermaxes, inmates rarely have access to educational or religious materials and services. Almost all toiletries (e.g., toothpaste, shaving cream, and razors) are strictly controlled. When an inmate is removed from his cell, he typically has to kneel down with his back to the door. Then he is required to place his hands through the food slot in the door to be handcuffed.

In spite of these simple facilities and the fact that prisoners' rehabilitation is not encouraged (and is next to impossible under these conditions), Supermax prisons are more expensive to build and to run than traditional prisons.

Prisoners are sentenced or transferred to Supermaxes for a variety of reasons that often boil down to a judge's sentence, classification processes, and inmates' behavior while they are incarcerated.

Officially, prison systems design classification categories as a means to designate prisoners to different security levels. Typically, the hard-core, violent convicts serving long sentences are assigned to maximum-security facilities; the incorrigible prisoners serving medium-length sentences are sentenced to medium-security prisons; and the relatively lightweight men serving short sentences are sentenced to minimum-security camps, farms, or community facilities.

For some convicts, the decision of where they will be sent is made long before they hop on their very first prison van. In the sentencing phase of a trial, the judge may specify where the convict will spend his or her time. For example, Ramzi Yousef, the convicted bomber in the 1993 attack on the World Trade Center, was sent directly to the federal Supermax in Florence, Colorado. Depending on sentencing guidelines and an individual's criminal history, officials must determine which security level is most appropriate for each convict. Alternatively, prisoners who are new to the system will be transferred to a receiving and departure setting, where they are classified into the appropriate receiving facility. . . .

Where a convict is sent depends on a number of factors. The division of probation and parole usually prepares a Pre-Sentence Investigation, which is another attempt by the criminal justice system to collect a prisoner's personal information. The probation or parole officer reviews a number of factors relevant to the convict's circumstances, including criminal history. They prepare a report, which makes a recommendation as to which facility would best suit the particular criminal. This report is then shared with the judge, defense attorney, and prosecutor—and the judge retains the ability to accept or dismiss the recommendation. By the same token, some well-heeled and high-profile defendants (e.g., Martha Stewart) or their loved ones may employ the services of sentencing consultants like Herb Hoelter of the National Center for Institutions and Alternatives. For a hefty fee, these hired individuals can prepare a report that recommends where a client should be sentenced. The defendant's attorney then passes the report on to the prosecutor (and judge) in hopes that it may ultimately influence the presiding judge.

In most lock-ups and prisons, the majority of the inmates do not get into trouble because they follow the rules. The problem population comprises approximately 1 percent of the prisoners in an institution. When there is an incident, such as a stabbing on a tier, correctional officers cannot place all of the suspects on administrative segregation (i.e., "in the hole"). But when this type of extreme punishment becomes the norm for a particular prisoner, the administration is usually prompted to transfer the inmate to a higher-security prison. Over time, a prisoner who repeatedly finds himself in this type of situation becomes more and more likely to end up at a Supermax facility.

Effects of Incarceration

All told, the isolation, lack of meaningful activity, and shortage of human contact take their toll on prisoners. Supermax residents often develop severe psychological disorders, though, unfortunately, we do not have specific psychological data, per se, on individuals kept in these facilities. However, numerous reports based on anecdotal information have documented the detrimental effects of these facilities.

The conditions inside Supermax prisons have led several corrections and human rights experts and organizations (like Amnesty International and the American Civil Liberties Union) to question whether these prisons are a violation of (1) the Eighth Amendment of the U.S. Constitution, which prohibits the state from engaging in cruel and unusual punishment, and/or (2) the European Convention on Human Rights and the United Nations' Universal Declaration of Human Rights, which were established to protect the rights of all individuals, whether living free or incarcerated. . . .

Supermax prisons have plenty of downsides, and not just as far as the inmates are concerned. Some individuals have suggested that Supermax prisons are all part of the correctional industrial complex (i.e., an informal network of correctional workers, professional organizations, and corporations that keep the jails and prisons system growing). Most of the Supermaxes in the United States are brand new or nearly so. Others are simply freestanding prisons that were retrofitted. According to a study by the Urban Institute, the annual per-cell cost of a Supermax is about $75,000, compared to $25,000 for each cell in an ordinary state prison.

Future Prospects

The United States has plenty of super-expensive Supermax facilities—two-thirds of the states now have them. But these facilities were designed when crime was considered a growing problem; the current lower violent-crime rate shows no real sign of a turn for the worse. However, as good as these prisons are at keeping our worst offenders in check, the purpose of the Supermax is in flux.

No self-respecting state director of corrections or correctional planner will admit that the Supermax concept was a mistake. And you would be wrong to think that these prisons can be replaced by something drastically less costly. But prison experts are beginning to realize that, just like a shrinking city that finds itself with too many schools or fire departments, the Supermax model must be made more flexible in order to justify its size and budget. . . .

Converting cells is one approach, but not the only one. Other ideas include building more regional Supermaxes and filling them by shifting populations from other states. This would allow administrators to completely empty out a given Supermax, and then close it down or convert it to another use.

There is also the possibility that some elements of the Supermax model could be combined with the approaches of more traditional prisons, creating a hybrid that serves a wider population. But different types of prisoners would have to be kept well away from each other—a logistical problem of no small concern.

The invention and adoption of Supermax prisons is perhaps the most significant indictment of the way we run correctional facilities and/or what we accomplish in correctional facilities. Most relatively intelligent people know that the United States incarcerates more people per capita than any other advanced industrialized country. And the average American rarely questions this fact. Then again, many people believe that individuals doing time are probably guilty anyway. Thus reforming or changing prisons is and will remain a constant struggle.

Redesigned Prisons Provide Humane Environments for Inmates

Richard Wener

Richard Wener is a professor of environmental psychology at the Polytechnic Institute of New York University.

In 1974, when the New York and Chicago Metropolitan Correctional Centers (MCCs) accepted their first inmates, the direct supervision system of correctional design and management (DS) was new and startlingly innovative. The appearance, the openness of these institutions, and the level of direct contact between staff and inmates is still surprising to many, especially those in the general public who have difficulty reconciling images of these new institutions with popular stereotypes of jails and prisons. Today direct supervision has become the face of modern, state-of-the-art corrections in hundreds of settings, and is accepted as best practice by professional and accrediting organizations, including the American Correctional Association and American Jail Association, the U.S. Bureau of Prisons [BOP], and many state and local corrections departments. . . .

There are five sometimes overlapping issues that might be identified as the evolutionary steps that became the qualities most identified as special to direct supervision: the change in the role of the officer; the placement of the officer within the living unit, in contact with inmates; the decentralization of functions to the living units; the decision to apply "soft architecture" to inmate units; and the development of a formal set of principles for managing these systems.

Richard Wener, "Direct Supervision—Evolution and Revolution," *American Jails*, March/April 2006, pp. 21–24. Copyright © 2006 American Jails Association. Reproduced by permission.

A New Understanding of the Role of the Officer in the Institution

One of the important changes in modern corrections has been the evolution of the basic institutional position from that of "guard" to "corrections officer." More than a semantic nicety, this new term reflects a change of the role and function of the security staff toward an increasing focus on the use of communication and counseling skills in dealing with inmates. In modern corrections, the officer is typically viewed as "a professional in security procedures, people management, and conflict resolution." Before this, officers typically were poorly trained and held in low esteem. They were the brute force that maintained order in prison systems.

Direct supervision has become the face of modern, state-of-the-art corrections in hundreds of settings.

In the mid-20th century, however, officers and other security staff were increasingly being trained in communication and counseling skills and employed as counselors or quasi-counselors in juvenile facilities, such as in experimental "open institutions" in Seagoville, Texas, and Alderson, West Virginia. Officers there were expected to use their abilities as counselors and group leaders to keep control, rather than weapons or barriers. The professionalization of the role of the officer was supported and promoted by unions and by the efforts of major institutions, including the National Institute of Justice (NIJ), the National Institute of Corrections (NIC) and the American Correctional Association (ACA). The role of the officer as a corrections professional was further promoted by the development of unit management.

Decentralized Small Living Units—Functional Unit Management

Within the BOP functional trait management was seen as the real and important innovation in corrections management. Its goal was to decentralize management and reduce the scale of the inmate population by dividing inmates into smaller groups, making it possible to maximize flexibility of programming and bring consistent supervision and services to the inmate. Functional units brought the various people and parts of inmate services together at the point where service was provided. As that happened the security officers who worked on those units naturally became an increasingly important part of the treatment team. Unit management also minimized the often dangerous and time consuming task of inmate transportation. Most importantly, though, it created smaller inmate groups for better social interaction and a more humane environment. . . .

One of the important changes in modern corrections has been the evolution of the basic institutional position from that of "guard" to "corrections officer."

By 1970, when planning for the MCCs was beginning, the concept was fully entrenched in bureau plans. The idea of taking officers out of control rooms and putting them in the living areas, in direct contact with inmates, went along hand-in-hand with the development of unit management.

Taking Officers Out of Control Rooms and Placing Them in the Living Area with Inmates

For most of corrections history the place of the corrections officer was outside looking in, maintaining control with hard barriers, surveillance, and force. As the BOP began to experiment with "open institutions" in which inmates had more freedom of movement, there was increased contact between inmates and officers. . . . While these ideas held sway in the central BOP office, many wardens were still concerned about this system and complained of the risk of serious violence and inmate takeovers. In state and county facilities officers almost always remained stationed in locked, barred control stations, separated from inmates except during movement, search, etc.

For some planners and administrators, pulling officers out of control rooms was unnerving. Some who were uncomfortable with the MCC model chose instead a halfway solution for their new facilities, which became known as "podular indirect supervision." While these jails had small living areas that resembled direct supervision units, inmates were remotely observed from an enclosed officer station. Others chose direct supervision but hedged their bets, by reducing the number of inmates in the living unit, as at the Manhattan House of Detention. Even with this modification, the head of the New York City correctional officer's union confidently predicted that inmates would destroy the space and attack the officers. This jail, in fact, became a model of smooth and safe operations.

If you provide inmates with humane settings and expect civil behavior from them, the result will be a better and safer environment.

The Use of Non-Institutional–Normalized Environment

Another striking element of the MCCs was the use of non-institutional fixtures, furnishings and materials. In many ways these design features represented an application of concepts from social and environmental psychology. These facilities, quite overtly and consciously, were created to maximize the power of expectations (set through social as well as physical symbols) to encourage positive behavioral norms. They provided "soft," flexible materials and furnishings to encourage caretaking among users. The designs were, in many cases, bright and colorful. The MCCs had carpets on floors and used light, upholstered furniture. Many fixtures were not hardened and vandal proof, but sometimes quite light and breakable.

These design elements were not inherent in the unit management system, but do logically derive from this and other trends, such as the push in the late 1960s for reintegration of prisoners into society after incarceration. One way to promote reintegration was to fight institutionalization and prisonization, such as by recreating prison environments with more normal symbols and settings. This philosophy promoted increased use of single rooms to provide privacy and reduce regimentation. It led planners to provide a perceptibly more "normal" setting, with bright colors on walls and furniture, carpeted floors, upholstered chairs, doors instead of bars, and windows to the outside.

Planners hoped that normal fixtures would be treated well by inmates. [Robert] Sommer had noted that "the architecture of the isolation cell is based on a variant of Murphy's Law—if something can be destroyed, it will be destroyed." He observed that if designers "challenge people to destroy something . . . they will find a way to do it" and commented that hard architecture is "costly, dehumanizing, and it isn't effective." He noted that inmates usually did not destroy objects indiscriminately in riots, and that things that were highly valued were likely to be treated more respectfully.

All the MCCs made special efforts to include bright colors, and non-institutional fixtures, furniture, and materials. In some cases this directive was taken to surprising extremes, such as the light fixtures in inmate rooms of the Chicago MCC that consisted of bare frosted bulbs that would have been considered fragile even in residential settings.

Defining the System and Identifying Underlying Management Principles

The new MCCs were not immediately copied. Direct supervision design and operation was simply too radical for many, especially in state and local jurisdictions. Some doubted that the MCC experience was relevant to what they thought were tougher and more hardcore local inmates. Many credit the "selling" of the MCC concept to W. R. Nelson, who was the first warden of the Chicago MCC and later Chief of the National Institute of Corrections Jails Division. Nelson re-labeled the system as "podular direct supervision," which better described for many in local settings the most unique aspects of the approach—placing the officer in discrete, open, living areas.

More importantly he also identified a series of management principles that were critical to successful operation of this approach. These principles are a mixture of elements that are basic to good management in any correctional setting (or most other administrative situations, for that matter) and issues that are particularly critical to making this approach work. These include maintaining "effective control" (being completely in charge of the environment, eliminating areas of "de facto" inmate control); providing "effective supervision" with personal interaction as well as surveillance; selecting and training competent staff; maintaining safety for staff and inmates; operating cost-effectively; teaching and practicing good communications between staff and inmates and among staff; correctly classifying inmates and orienting them to the new situation; and enforcing rules in a manner seen to be clearly fair and impartial. . . .

The ideas that were embodied in the MCCs, even though radical in the context of 1970s jail design and management, evolved from a series of operational and design changes that took place over several decades, mostly within the Bureau of Prisons. These changes began in small steps that addressed how inmates were classified and grouped, how officers were used and trained, and eventually how spaces were organized and designed. As important as some of the individual steps were, however, the whole became much more than the sum of its parts. The most radical aspect of unit management and direct supervision was that they ultimately challenged and changed underlying assumptions that served as the basis of correctional operations. They altered the essential understanding of who inmates are, how they can be expected to behave, and how they will respond to different kinds of treatment. In so doing they have created opportunities for better, more humane, and more effective correctional systems. There is a long way to go—many correctional settings within and outside the U.S. reflect outmoded, ineffective, unprofessional, and sometimes brutal and inhumane forms of treatment. There are now, however, many successful examples of institutions that operate on notions that many people once thought of as naïve—notions that suggest that if you provide inmates with humane settings and expect civil behavior from them, the result will be a better and safer evironment. This remains one of the most hopeful aspects of modern correctional design and operations.

Dog-Training Programs in Prisons Give Inmates Second Chances

Matthew Schniper

Matthew Schniper is the culture editor for the Colorado Springs Independent.

In 1996, at the age of 20, Robert Gerle landed in prison. A series of felonies had climaxed in an aggravated assault charge when he took a police officer's gun and left him bound by his own handcuffs.

At a time when most people are just beginning their adult lives, Gerle found himself at something of an ending. A 24-year sentence in front of him, it was difficult to imagine how he would fill his days.

Within a few years, Gerle began teaching math and science inside Arrowhead Correctional Center's GED program in Cañon City. He gained satisfaction from helping other inmates, but after 3 years, it was waning.

Around that time, a rumor began circulating that the "dog program" was coming to Arrowhead. Gerle didn't get too excited. As he points out, "99.9 percent of prison rumors are complete horse hockey."

Then a transferred inmate showed up from the nearby Territorial Correctional Facility. He'd been in the dog program there and soon would be helping facilitate one at Arrowhead—or so Gerle heard.

It wasn't until minor renovations began on one wing of cells on the living unit, with bunks raised to fit kennels and a potty yard constructed outside, that Gerle believed there'd soon be dogs bounding about. Along with many others who

Matthew Schniper, "Sit, Stay, Start Over," *Colorado Spring Independent*, February 14, 2008. Copyright © 2008 Colorado Springs Independent. Reproduced by permission.

met the prerequisites—six months of good behavior, possession of a diploma or GED, and non-sex offender status—he submitted a formal application to join the Prison Trained K-9 Companion Program.

The program would rescue dogs from shelters and desperate situations, vaccinate them and then spay or neuter them. At that point, they'd be turned over to inmates to train for sale as companion service, search and rescue or explosive-detection dogs. The process would take anywhere from a month to the better part of a year for the specialized dogs.

Within a month, Gerle underwent an intensive interview with program supervisor and founder Debi Stevens, and a panel of Department of Corrections (DOC) heads. A few hours afterward, he ran into Stevens on his way to the chow hall and stopped to thank her for the interview. She replied with a curt, "Well, don't disappoint me."

The comment hung in the air for a moment, he says, before she cracked a thin smile and said, "That's my way of saying congratulations. You're accepted into the program."

Two days later, Gerle moved into his new living unit, and a week or so after that, a vanload of dogs appeared at the prison's gates. That was the day Gerle met Skye, a border collie with one dark brown eye and one bright blue eye.

As they grow more skilled with each run through the course, the dogs build confidence. So do the men.

Upon arrival, Gerle says Skye hopped down from Stevens' van, walked up to six anxious inmates and sniffed, turning up her nose at each. Upon reaching his feet, she sniffed, cocked her head to the side and plopped down. He'd been chosen.

"I was giddy," recalls Gerle, who'd grown up with pets and considered losing them one of the most traumatic aspects of prison. "I felt like it was the first day in school, first date, all that, combined into one." I'd been eight years since he'd pet a dog. For some of the other trainers, it had been more than 20.

How It Works

On a cold, early January morning, 36-year-old Marion Crawford and his dog for the month, Lucky, stand alongside his teammates and their dogs against the fence of a K-9 agility course outside his cellblock in Territorial Correctional Facility. Above the men, giant spools of barbed wire line a wall of rock quarried from the scarred mountainside behind the prison.

Before Crawford has a chance to show off Lucky's hula hoop-jumping skills—impressive for a silky terrier—Kenneth Cobbin leads his rust-colored Vizsla, named Copper, up and down a ramp, through some obstacles, across a balance beam and finally over a seesaw.

Though the dogs appear at play, their routines are really the culmination of weeks of obedience training. The dogs keep dually focused on the impediments before them and their trainer's commands. As they grow more skilled with each run through the course, the dogs build confidence. So do the men.

Across Cañon City at the Colorado Women's Correctional Facility, an average day of work on the Prison Trained K-9 Companion Program is also under way. The program is similarly in action nearby at the Arrowhead Correctional Center. In Buena Vista, Trinidad, Fort Lyon, Sterling and the Denver Women's facility as in a privately run prison in Brush, the scene is roughly the same.

This program saves dogs' lives, and it changes inmates' lives.

Because of its success in many arenas, Colorado Correctional Industries, a non-tax-supported division of the DOC, has essentially franchised its dog program. What began in October 2002 with five dogs and five handlers at the women's facility has grown into a program of 130 inmates spread across the nine minimum- and medium-security facilities.

"This program saves dogs' lives, and it changes inmates' lives," says Stevens. "It teaches them new life skills. Some people never even learned how to get up in the morning and go to work. One of the things that happens in prison is all an inmate can see is 'me-me-me,'. . . up there on that block [are] 14 men that have to learn to work together."

Today, the program also accepts "boarding-in" dogs from people who are tired of wrestling with behavioral issues. The money that the DOC charges those folks keeps the program afloat.

It's the companionship, and "somebody who loves you unconditionally," . . . that make the work worthwhile.

It's the companionship, and "somebody who loves you unconditionally," according to Crawford, that make the work worthwhile. And it's the simple occurrence that brings light to the otherwise staid environment. For many inmates, the best part of the day is what had been one of the worst—wake-up call.

Crawford, his face lighting up in the retelling, says that each morning the dogs wake up just before the inmates and sit obediently in their kennels, awaiting the morning bell. As soon as it rings and the lights blink on, the dogs scamper wildly out of the kennels and jump into the inmates' beds to say good morning. "It's lovely," says Crawford. "It happens every day."

After the ritual, the real work begins. The inherent irony in it: People who've been locked up because they seemingly didn't know how to behave properly in society are training dogs to do just that.

'It's a Job'

Gerle quickly learned the program involves much more than just teaching the dogs to sit or roll over. Many dogs end up in the program because of serious behavior problems, and they require hours of repetition, reinforcement and trust-building to reshape their behavior.

People who've been locked up because they seemingly didn't know how to behave properly in society are training dogs to do just that.

Inmates are often up in the middle of the night, taking their dogs out or tending to them if they're sick. They contact Stevens if a problem seems serious, but themselves learn to administer heartworm preventatives and vaccinations, and closely monitor the dogs' behaviors for signs of need. They learn dog-speak, so to speak.

In the words of 49-year-old Cobbin, serving a life sentence for armed robbery: "It's not a pet. It's a job."

The specialized skill earns dog trainers $2 per day, along with incentive bonuses; the average offender makes only 60 cents a day. Aside from the canteen money, and something positive to do, the program yields inmates a master trainer's certificate and the option to earn an associate degree in canine behavior modification from the Colorado community-college system.

On a typical day, an inmate will train a dog with the whole class for a couple hours in the morning and then continue one-on-one training, sometimes using the agility course, for another hour in the afternoon. The dogs stay with their hosts 24 hours a day, getting constant behavioral reinforcement.

"We worked as a team not only to train, but to help each other keep from letting frustrations mount to the point that they were overwhelming to us," Gerle says. "We learned to keep our tempers in check and our mouths under control, which is not a common thing in prison." If one trainer saw another becoming agitated, he'd offer to take the guy's dog for a few minutes so he could relax or blow off steam.

"We can critically analyze something, but a dog can't," Gerle says. "All they know is they failed and that you're not happy. You've gotta set them up to succeed." If you ask Stevens, or just about anybody connected to the K-9 program, you'd hear that's what the DOC has in mind for the inmates, too. . . .

Though inspired in part by a search-and-rescue dog-training program at Burlington's Kit Carson Correctional Facility, the Prison Trained K-9 Companion Program was not actually modeled after any predecessor. In fact, other correctional folks have joined a wait list for a K-9 behavioral modification textbook that CCI's print shop is wrapping up. CCI has even hosted international visitors from places like Russia and Japan who've come to study this and other programs inside Colorado's prison system.

The dogs stay with their hosts 24 hours a day, getting constant behavioral reinforcement.

Second Chances

When Lori McLuckie, 46, was first accepted into the K-9 program, she'd been in prison 14 years. It had been so long since she'd nurtured something that she was afraid she was going "to break" her dog.

Seated in the corner of a drab conference room, a Dachshund mix in her lap, McLuckie speaks softly and chooses her words deliberately. "It opens you up," she says, "and you tend to close up in here. When you first come to the program . . . you feel kinda raw for a while."

McLuckie, in for life on a murder charge, was one of the first five handlers to launch the dog program at the women's correctional facility. It didn't take long for her to grow into it.

Last spring, she was assigned a blind and deaf, mixed-breed dog named Gracie. On her own, the trainer ultimately devised a system based on a combination of scent and touch.

She would stomp a foot next to Gracie so the dog could feel the brush of air and vibration on the floor to communicate the sit, stay or disciplinary commands and appeal to Gracie's nose—all dogs' primary sensory unit—with treats. "[It was] the most awesome thing I've ever seen," says fellow inmate Bertha Martinez.

The best part of her work, McLuckie says, is the awareness that she's helping the dogs and people that receive them. By reshaping dogs' behaviors, she gives them a better chance of "fitting in" with a family so that they avoid ending up in a shelter again.

People who under any other circumstances would never speak to each other ..., including members of different gangs, would come up to each other and talk about the dogs.

She, like all the inmates, needs to believe in second chances. "I think everybody deserves that, even humans," says Cobbin. "[Giving the dogs a second chance is] like saving a life. I don't know how you can explain that feeling." ...

All of which is wonderful, but relevant to administrators only if the safety of every person and dog in the program can be assured. Convincing security managers to allow crates, leashes, training collars and other necessities—all potential weapons—in a tightly controlled environment took some patient back-and-forths. "One slip in the early days, and we were gone," says Stevens.

But positive feedback came almost immediately. Prison staff from various areas reported that tensions system-wide went down as soon as the dogs arrived in each facility. According to Gerle, people who under any other circumstances would never speak to each other or even acknowledge each other's presence, including members of different gangs, would come up to each other and talk about the dogs.

"There's not very many [situations] in prison where you can look at the other person and just see a person," Stevens says. "The dogs open that door. They make you both people."

She adds that staff members who were initially against "rewarding inmates by giving them dogs" later came to her to talk about how surprised they were at certain inmates' improved behaviors and attitudes. Others have noted "pro-social stabilization" benefits that make the inmates easier to manage.

Nowadays, [DOC Director of Public Relations Katherine] Sanguinetti says, DOC staffers who transfer from a prison with the K-9 program to one without often promote it and petition their superiors to bring it in.

To date, Stevens and Sanguinetti say no major problems have occurred inside the program. "The inmates police it," says Sanguinetti. "They don't want one of their peers to blow it for all of them."

"Yeah," adds Stevens, "I wouldn't want to be the inmate who caused the dog program to be closed."

Breaking the Cycle

Now 32, Robert Gerle is out on intensive supervision parole in metro Denver, having been released into a halfway house in November 2006 and paroled in April 2007. He wears a bracelet that monitors his movements, but he has earned limited freedoms such as a relaxed curfew and driving privileges to work, church and meetings with his parole officer.

Gerle stands out as a success for his thus-far successful transition back into society—especially considering the state's recidivism rate is 49.8 percent, according to the DOC's latest three-year study.

Shortly after landing at the halfway house, Gerle scored a job as a pet training instructor at PetSmart, which he held until March 2007. Since then, he's worked as a client-service representative for a 24-hour emergency veterinary center. He says he was up-front about his background, and both businesses were willing to look past his rap sheet to his qualifications.

At the emergency facility, Gerle says he's able to do a little more basic veterinary care and triage than other staff members, due to his experience. In addition, he's the go-to-guy for "feisty" animals that come in, again noting skills and techniques he learned inside the K-9 program.

Gerle also does some private training; out of 40 or so folks he's worked with at least once, only one has expressed discomfort with his background.

Many inmates say they never cared for anyone or anything outside prison, but now they feel proud to take care of the dogs.

He likes to believe that when the general public sees inmates working hard to save dogs that, in many cases, were steps away from euthanization—that they are changing behavior patterns and creating good companions—perhaps they'll say, "Maybe, maybe, they're not so bad. Maybe there's some redeeming qualities in some of these folks who happen to be locked up for making bad decisions."

That is how Martinez, 30 years old and in for up to 50 years on murder and robbery, hopes society will view her. "You don't see what I'm here for," she says, "you see what I'm doing."

K-9 Companion program instructor Edward Shallufy says he's heard many inmates say they never cared for anyone or anything outside prison, but now they feel proud to take care of the dogs.

"It's really strange to see a 300-pound guy with muscles bigger than my neck get down on his knees with sweet talk and baby talk . . . caring for [the dogs] when they're sick . . ."

Gerle understands there will be plenty of skeptics. To them, he points out that most people—95 to 97 percent, according to Sanguinetti—will get out of prison someday.

"Do we want them to get out having this attitude that the entire world is against them, or out with some education and skills that will allow them to become the proverbial productive members of society?" he asks. "The dogs were, and continue to be, the single best ambassador between inmates and staff, and between inmates and the public, that we could possibly ask for."

"No matter how well I present myself, I don't have four legs and a tail."

Organizations to Contact

The editors have compiled the following list of organizations concerned with the issues debated in this book. The descriptions are derived from materials provided by the organizations. All have publications or information available for interested readers. The list was compiled on the date of publication of the present volume; names, addresses, and phone numbers may change. Be aware that many organizations take several weeks or longer to respond to inquiries, so allow as much time as possible.

American Jail Association (AJA)
1135 Professional Ct., Hagerstown, MD   21740-5853
(301) 790-3930
Web site: www.aja.org

The AJA is a national, nonprofit organization dedicated to supporting those who work in and operate the nation's jails. It publishes *American Jails* magazine and *Exploring Jail Operations*, a book that can be purchased in PDF format from its Web site.

Citizens Alliance on Prisons and Public Spending (CAPPS)
403 Seymour Ave., Suite 200, Lansing, MI   48933
(517) 482-7753 • Fax: (517) 482-7754
E-mail: capps@capps-mi.org
Web site: www.capps-mi.org

CAPPS is a nonprofit public policy organization concerned about the social and economic costs of prison expansion. It opposes the incarceration of criminals who pose no risk to society. Its Web site presents extensive information about how and why prison populations should be reduced, plus profiles of specific prisoners that it believes should be paroled.

Commission on Safety and Abuse in America's Prisons

1330 Connecticut Ave. NW, Suite B, Washington, DC   20036
(202) 347-6776 • Fax: (202) 347-6047
E-mail: info@prisoncommission.org
Web site: www.prisoncommission.org

In 2005–2006 the Commission on Safety and Abuse in America's Prisons explored violence and abuse in America's prisons and jails in an effort to determine how to make correctional facilities safer for prisoners and staff and more effective in promoting public safety and public health. Its report, *Confronting Confinement*, and transcripts of public hearings can be downloaded from its Web site.

Corrections Connection Network News (CCNN)

159 Burgin Parkway, Quincy, MA   02169
(617) 471 4445 • Fax: (617) 770 3339
Web site: www.corrections.com

CCNN offers news and other information to corrections professionals. Its Web site contains newsletter and Ezine archives plus articles on many topics related to prisons and an extensive list of links to other relevant sites.

Corrections Corporation of America (CCA)

10 Burton Hills Blvd., Nashville, TN   37215
(800) 624-2931 • Fax: (615) 263-3140
Web site: www.correctionscorp.com

CCA is the nation's industry leader of privately managed corrections solutions for federal, state, and local governments. Its Web site offers information about the advantages of private prisons and about the specific prisons it operates.

Families Against Mandatory Minimums (FAMM)

1612 K St. NW, Suite 700, Washington, DC   20006
(202) 822-6700 • Fax: (202) 822-6704
Web site: www.famm.org

FAMM is a national voice for fair and proportionate sentencing laws. It advocates state and federal sentencing reform and aims to mobilize thousands of individuals and families whose lives are adversely affected by unjust sentences. Its Web site contains information about sentencing and profiles of individuals it believes have been unjustly sentenced.

Federal Bureau of Prisons
320 First St. NW, Washington, DC   20534
(202) 307-3198
Web site: www.bop.gov

The Federal Bureau of Prisons is responsible for the custody and care of federal offenders. Its Web Site contains extensive information about federal prisons, articles on prison management published by the Bureau, and search facilities through which any federal inmate can be located.

Pew Center on the States
901 E St. NW, 10th Floor, Washington, DC   20004-1409
(202) 552-2000 • Fax: (202) 552-2299
Web site: www.pewcenteronthestates.org

The Pew Center on the States works to advance state policies that serve the public interest. It conducts credible research, brings together diverse perspectives, and analyzes states' experiences to determine what works and what does not. Its two major reports on prisons, *One in 100: Behind Bars in America* (2008) and *One in 31: The Long Reach of American Corrections* (2009), can be downloaded from its Web site.

Private Corrections Institute (PCI)
1114 Brandt Dr., Tallahassee, FL   32308
Web site: www.privateci.org

The mission of the PCI is to stop the trend of privatizing correctional institutions and services by providing information and assistance to citizens, policy makers, and journalists concerning the dangers and pitfalls of this trend. Its Web site contains news and other material critical of the private prison industry.

Puppies Behind Bars
10 East 40th St., 19th Floor, New York, NY   10016
(212) 680-9562 • Fax: (212) 689-9330
Web site: www.puppiesbehindbars.com

Puppies Behind Bars trains inmates to raise puppies to become service dogs for the disabled and explosive detection canines for law enforcement. Its Web site answers frequently asked questions about the program, plus it features a video showing how inmates interact with their dogs.

Real Cost of Prisons Project (RCPP)
Lois Ahrens, 5 Warfield Pl., Northampton, MA   01060
E-mail: lois@realcostofprisons.org
Web site: realcostofprisons.org

The RCPP brings together justice activists, artists, justice policy researchers, and people directly experiencing the impact of mass incarceration to create popular education materials and other resources that explore the immediate and long-term costs of incarceration on the individual, her/his family, the community, and the nation. Its Web site contains essays by prisoners, links to many articles about prisons, and information about the comic books it publishes.

The Sentencing Project
514 Tenth St. NW, Suite 1000, Washington, DC   20004
(202) 628-0871 • Fax: (202) 628-1091
E-mail: staff@sentencingproject.org
Web site: www.sentencingproject.org

The Sentencing Project is a national organization working for a fair and effective criminal justice system by promoting reforms in sentencing law and practice, and alternatives to incarceration. It publishes policy reports, briefing sheets, and educational materials on a wide range of criminal justice issues. The organization hosts noteworthy research, litigation materials, and commentary from some of the nation's foremost experts on criminal justice policy and civil rights.

U.S. Department of Justice Bureau of Justice Statistics (BJS)
810 Seventh St. NW, Washington, DC   20531
(202) 307-0765
Web site: www.ojp.usdoj.gov/bjs/prisons.htm

The BJS mission is to collect, analyze, publish, and disseminate information on crime, criminal offenders, victims of crime, and the operation of justice systems at all levels of government. The BJS Web site provides extensive detailed statistical reports on crime, prisons, and inmates.

Vera Institute of Justice
233 Broadway, 12th Floor, New York, NY   10279
(212) 334-1300 • Fax: (212) 941-9407
E-mail: contactvera@vera.org
Web site: www.vera.org

The Vera Institute of Justice combines expertise in research, demonstration projects, and technical assistance to help leaders in government and civil society improve the systems people rely on for justice and safety. Many of its publications, including *Widening the Lens 2008: A Panoramic View of Juvenile Justice in New York State*, can be downloaded from its Web site.

Bibliography

Books

Sasha Abramsky — *American Furies: Crime, Punishment, and Vengeance in the Age of Mass Imprisonment*. Boston: Beacon Press, 2008.

Lois Ahrens, Craig Gilmore, and Kevin Pyle — *The Real Cost of Prisons Comix*. Oakland, CA: PM Press, 2008.

Curtis R. Blakely — *America's Prisons: The Movement Toward Profit and Privatization*. Boca Raton, FL: Brown Walker Press, 2005.

James H. Bruton — *The Big House: Life Inside a Supermax Security Prison*. Stillwater, MN: Voyageur, 2004.

Bill Dallas and George Barna — *Lessons from San Quentin: Everything I Needed to Know About Life I Learned in Prison*. Carol Stream, IL: Tyndale House, 2009.

Mark Dow — *American Gulag: Inside U.S. Immigration Prisons*. Berkeley: University of California Press, 2004.

Alan Elsner — *Gates of Injustice: The Crisis in America's Prisons*. Upper Saddle River, NJ: Prentice Hall, 2006.

Jennifer Gonnerman — *Life on the Outside: The Prison Odyssey of Elaine Bartlett*. New York: Farrar, Straus and Giroux, 2004.

Marie Gottschalk — *The Prison and the Gallows: The Politics of Mass Incarceration in America.* New York: Cambridge University Press, 2006.

Michael A. Hallett — *Private Prisons in America: A Critical Race Perspective.* Urbana: University of Illinois Press, 2006.

Victor Hassine — *Life Without Parole: Living in Prison Today.* New York: Oxford University Press, 2003.

Tara J. Herivel and Paul Wright, eds. — *Prison Profiteers: Who Makes Money from Mass Incarceration.* New York: New Press, 2008.

Michael Jacobson — *Downsizing Prisons: How to Reduce Crime and End Mass Incarceration.* New York: New York University Press, 2005.

Christian Parenti — *Lockdown America: Police and Prisons in the Age of Crisis.* New York: Verso, 2008.

T.J. Parsell — *Fish: A Memoir of a Boy Inside a Man's Prison.* New York: Carroll & Graf, 2006.

Steven Rafael and Michael A. Stoll, eds. — *Do Prisons Make Us Safer?: The Benefits and Costs of the Prison Boom.* New York: Russell Sage Foundation, 2009.

Lorna A. Rhodes — *Total Confinement: Madness and Reason in the Maximum Security Prison.* Berkeley: University of California Press, 2004.

Michael G. Santos *Inside: Life Behind Bars in America.* New York: St. Martin's, 2006.

Jens Soering *An Expensive Way to Make Bad People Worse: An Essay on Prison Reform from an Insider's Perspective.* New York: Lantern Books, 2004.

Silja J.A. Talvi *Women Behind Bars: The Crisis of Women in the U.S. Prison System.* Emeryville, CA: Seal Press, 2007.

Bruce Western *Punishment and Inequality in America.* New York: Russell Sage Foundation, 2007.

Franklin E. Zimring *The Great American Crime Decline.* New York: Oxford University Press, 2007.

Periodicals

Peter Aldhous "Throwing Away the Key," *New Scientist*, Feb. 24, 2007.

Joseph Berger "Prison Puppies," *New York Times*, June 1, 2008.

Leon Botstein "Con Ed," *New Republic*, Mar. 18, 2009.

Jason Cohen "Yes in My Backyard!" *Texas Monthly*, September 2004.

Jim Dwyer "Less Crime: No Reason to Shut Prisons," *New York Times*, Apr. 12, 2008.

Kai Falkenberg   "Time Off for Bad Behavior," *Forbes*, Jan. 12, 2009.

Atul Gawande   "Hellhole," *New Yorker*, Mar. 30, 2009.

Lauren E. Glaze   "Parents in Prison and Their Minor Children," *Bureau of Justice Statistics*, August 2008.

Marie Gottschalk   "The World's Warden: Crime, Punishment, and Politics in the United States," *Dissent*, Fall 2008.

Christine Hauser   "Marrying at Rikers: Few Frills, Many Rules," *New York Times*, May 10, 2008.

Glenn C. Loury   "Why Are So Many Americans in Prison? Race and the Transformation of Justice," *Boston Review*, July/August 2007.

Robert M. Maccarone   "Community Corrections and the Prison Rape Elimination Act," *Corrections Today*, October 2007.

Katherine Mason and Nina Williams-Mbengue   "A Different Kind of Jail," *State Legislatures*, December 2008.

Christopher Miller and Richard F. Southby   "From Arrest to Inmate to Release," *American Jails*, January/February 2007.

Brian Mockenhaupt   "The Tunnel," *Esquire*, August 2008.

Lisa D. Moore and Amy Elkavich	"Who's Using and Who's Doing Time," *American Journal of Public Health*, September 2008.
Solomon Moore	"The Prison Overcrowding Fix," *New York Times*, Feb. 10, 2009.
John Rosales	"Prison Drama," *NEA Today*, September 2007.
Beth Schwartzapfel	"Lullabies Behind Bars," *Ms.*, Fall 2008.
William Scism and Sterling Bryan	"Can Technology Address the Contraband Cell Phone Problem?" *Corrections Today*, October 2008.
Howard N. Snyder and Jeanne B. Stinchcomb	"Do Higher Incarceration Rates Mean Lower Crime Rates?" *Corrections Today*, October 2006.
James Sterngold	"Worst of the Worst," *Mother Jones*, July/August 2008.
Anthony A. Sterns, Greta Lax, Chad Sed, et al.	"The Growing Wave of Older Prisoners," *Corrections Today*, August 2008.
Christine Tartaro and Marissa P. Levy	"Crowding, Violence and Direct Supervision Jails," *American Jails*, September/October 2008.
Wendy G. Turner	"The Experiences of Offenders in a Prison Canine Program," *Federal Probation*, June 2007.
John Vratil and John Whitmire	"Cutting the Prison Rate Safely," *Washington Post*, Mar. 20, 2008.

Bruce Western   "The Prison Boom and the Decline of American Citizenship," *Society*, vol. 44, iss. 30, 2007.

Denise Kersten Wills   "An Inside Job," *Teacher Magazine*, May/June 2007.

James Q. Wilson   "Do the Time, Lower the Crime," *Los Angeles Times*, Mar. 30, 2008.

Andrew P. Wiper, Steffie Woolhandler, J. Wesley Boyd, et al.   "The Health and Health Care of U.S. Prisoners: Results of a Nationwide Survey," *American Journal of Public Health*, April 2009.

Index

A

ABC (television), 44

Abner, Carrie, 155–163

Abraham, Lynne, 145–146

Abu Ghraib, 86, 137

ACA (American Correctional Association), 93, 96, 130, 193–194

ACLU (American Civil Liberties Union), 92, 111, 113, 125

African American

    incarceration rates, 18, 25, 34, 44–45

    voting rights, 38

    women, 59

AFSCME (American Federation of State, County, and Municipal Employees), 131

Alabama Department of Corrections, 151

Albion Correctional Facility for Women, 71

Allen, George, 169

Allen, Richard, 154

Allenwood Federal Correctional Complex, 174–176, 178

AMA (American Medical Association), 92

American Bar Association, 92

American Civil Liberties Union (ACLU), 92, 111, 113, 125

American Conservative Union, 24

American Correctional Association (ACA), 93, 96, 130, 193–194

American Federation of State, County, and Municipal Employees (AFSCME), 131

American Humanist Association, 82

American Jail Association, 193

American Legislative Exchange Council, 170

American Medical Association (AMA), 92

American Notes (Dickens), 17

American Probation and Parole Association, 162

American Psychology-Law Society, 94

Americans United for Separation of Church and State, 83

Angola State Penitentiary, 161

Anno, Jaye, 94

Appignani Humanist Legal Center, 82

Aramark Correctional Services, 171

Arizona, 108–110, 140–143

Arizona Department of Corrections, 130

Arpaio, Joe, 108–113

Arrowhead Correctional Center, 200–203

Associated Press (AP), 122–125

Atlanta Magazine, 29

The Autobiography of Ben Franklin (Franklin), 166

B

Baca, Lee, 119
Barbour, Haley, 118
Bell, Dan, 65–72
Bender, William, 133–139
Benefield, Nathan, 126–132
Berman, Douglas, 181–182
BIS (Bureau of Justice Statistics), 69–70, 142, 170
Bittner, Terry, 153–154
BOP (U.S. Bureau of Prisons), 151, 193
Boredom, 176–177
Bright, Stephen, 33, 86–88
Brown, Jerry, 37
Bunton, Toni, 73–81
Bureau of Justice Assistance, 130
Bureau of Justice Statistics (BIS), 69–70, 142, 170
Bush, George H. W., 185
Bush, George W., 83

C

The Caged Melting Pot (Marquart), 101
California
    correctional healthcare, 90, 94, 123–125
    crime rate, 49
    criminal justice system, 47
    early release program, 118–119
    inmate forecasts, 48–49
    prison overcrowding, 115, 118, 120, 122–125
    prison population, 47–48, 124
    prison rape legislation, 71–72
    prison spending, 120, 124–125
    recidivism, 49–50
    three strikes statutes, 47–52, 124
    violent offenders, 49–50
California Department of Corrections and Rehabilitation, 51, 98–99
Cate, Mathew, 125
CCA (Correctional Corporation of America), 170–171
CCI (Colorado Correctional Industries), 202, 205
CEC (Community Education Centers), 138–139
Cell phones, 148, 150–154
Cermak Health Services, 97
Chain gangs, 17
Chavez, R. Scott, 97
China, 22, 25
Chuck Colson's Prison Fellowship, 83–84
Citizen's Research Council, 121
City Journal, 45
Civil rights, 18, 57–58, 123
Class action lawsuits, 58
Clinton, Bill, 177
CNN News, 108
Colorado Correctional Industries (CCI), 202, 205
Colorado Women's Correctional Facility, 202
Commonwealth Foundation, 126
Community Education Centers (CEC), 138–139
Community-based programs, 19
Contract labor, 17–18, 26, 36
Control Handling Units (CHU), 183
Cook County Bureau of Health Services, 97

Cook County Jail, 97

Corporal punishment, 16, 57

Correctional Corporation of America (CCA), 170–171

Correctional Health Care: Guidelines for the Management of an Adequate Delivery System (Anno), 94

Correctional healthcare, 89–97

Corruption, 17, 116

Corzine, Jon, 120

Costello v. Wainwright, 141

Council of Prison Locals, 180

Crawford, Marion, 202–203

Crime rates, 26, 32–33, 40–42, 181–182

Criminal Justice Institute, 160

Criminal Justice Legal Foundation, 50

Criminal justice system, 35, 42, 47, 63

Culp, Richard, 138

D

Dallas County (Texas) jail, 90–91

Delaware County Board of Prison Inspectors, 138

DeLoche, James, 151–153

Democracy in America (Tocqueville), 37

Deterrence, 19, 26, 33, 46

Detroit Free Press (newspaper), 73

Detroit Recorder's Court, 77

Dickens, Charles, 17

DiFilipo, Dana, 144–146

DiMascio, Bill, 146

Direct-supervision (DS) systems, 149, 193–197
    corrections officers, 194–196
    issues, qualities, 193

Dog training programs, 110, 137, 149
    Arrowhead Correction Center, 200–203
    Colorado Women's Correctional Facility, 202
    Kit Carson Correctional Facility, 205
    Prison Trained K-9 Companion Program, 202, 205, 208
    program feedback, 206–207
    Territorial Correction Center, 200, 202

Donald, James, 30–32

Donaldson Correctional Facility, 152–153

Draper Correctional Facility, 151–152

Drug abuse, 28, 76, 120, 128, 176

DS (direct-supervision) systems, 149, 193–197
    corrections officers, 194–196
    issues, qualities, 193

Dvoskin, Joel, 94–95

E

Earley, Mark, 172

Early release programs, 117–121, 148–149

Eastern State Penitentiary, 16–17

Education, 33, 36–37, 80, 138–139, 166–168

Eighth Amendment rights, 26, 57, 91, 103–104, 190

Elderly inmates, 176
    healthcare, 156–163, 171–172

programs, policies, 160–163
release programs, 162–163, 172
special needs, 158–160
trends, 155–156, 163
women, 159
Electronic monitoring, 19, 54–55, 116, 144–146
Elmore Correctional Center, 150, 152, 154
Employment, 17–18, 26, 32, 36
Estelle v. Gamble, 91–93
European Convention on Human Rights, 190

F

Families Against Mandatory Minimums, 181
Faulk, Dennis, 174
Federal Bureau of Prisons (FBOP), 174, 187
Federal Correctional Institution at Talladega, 150
Federal grants, 37
Federal Interagency Forum on Aging-Related Statistics, 156
Fennessy, Steve, 29–33
First Amendment rights, 84
Florida, 135, 140–143, 157
Food service, 103–107, 171
Franklin, Ben, 166
Fraser, David, 55

G

Gamble, Estelle v., 91–93
Gangs, 100, 149, 151
GEO Group, 133–139
George W. Hill Correctional Facility, 133, 138

Georgia, 29–31, 93, 162
Georgia Department of Corrections, 93
Gerle, Robert, 200–201, 203–209
Gillison, Everett, 144–145
Gingrich, Newt, 109
Global positioning system (GPS) tracking, 116, 144–146
Gonnerman, Jennifer, 34–38
Gorden, Robert, 150–154
Gordon, Claire, 25–28
Grace, Marianne, 134–135
Greenwood, Arin, 103–107

H

Hawaii, 63
Healthcare, 89–97, 123
Hiley, James, 108–113
HIV-AIDS, 95–96
Hocking Correctional Facility, 160
Hoelter, Herb, 189
Hoffman Hall, 139
Homicide rates, 26
Hoover Institution, 53
Hosier, John, 139
Hubbell, Webster, 177
Human Rights Watch (HRW), 65, 79

I

Incarceration
African Americans, 18, 25, 34, 44–45
China, 22, 25
costs, 22, 24–25, 31–32, 34, 39
early history, 16–17
Hispanic adults, 25
Michigan rates, 121
racial patterns, 64

rates, 22, 25–26, 29–30, 33, 39, 190–191
Russia, 36
Supermax prisons, 183–192
women, 60
Infectious diseases, 95–96
Inmate housing, 19, 98–100
Inmate lawsuits, 57–58, 85–89, 98
Costello v. Wainwright, 141
Estelle v. Gamble, 91–93
Maass v. LeMaire, 103–104
Nutraloaf, 103–107
prison overcrowding, 123
privatization, private prisons, 136
Turner v. Safley, 82
InnerChange Freedom Initiative, 84
Iowa Corrections Department, 83–84
ITT Corp., 153–154

J

Jacobsen, Michael, 39–43
Jail Project, AMA, 92
John Jay College of Criminal Justice, 138

K

Kaczynksi, Ted, 187
Kallenback, Fay, 133, 136
Keene, David, 24
King County Jail, Seattle, 60
Kit Carson Correctional Facility, 205
Klaas, Polly, 47
Kopczynski, Ken, 135

L

A Land Fit for Criminals (Fraser), 55
LeMaire v. Maass, 103–104
Life sentences, 168–170
Life-long learning, 166–168
Litigation. See inmate lawsuits
Lompac, 179
Long-term imprisonment, 16
Lowry, Bryan, 180
Luchenitser, Alex, 83
Luscome, Richard, 140–143

M

Maass, LeMaire v., 103–104
Male rape, 65–72
Mandatory minimum sentencing, 23, 30–32, 117, 121
Manhattan House of Detention, 196
Manhattan Institute, 44
Maricopa County Jail, 108–110, 140–143
Marquart, Jim, 101–102
Mauer, Mark, 117, 180
McCollum, Patrick, 85
MCCs (Metropolitan Correctional Centers)
design, 193–197
functional unit management, 194–196
management principles, 197–198
non-institutional-normalized environment use, 196–197
system design, 197–198
McDonnell, Robert, 170
McLuckie, Lori, 205–206
Media, media headlines, 44

Medical neglect, 64
Medium-security prisons, 19
Mental health services, 95
Mental illness, 27–28, 86, 90
Metropolitan Correctional Centers (MCCs)
    design, 193–197
    functional unit management, 194–196
    management principles, 197–198
    non-institutional-normalized environment use, 196–197
    system design, 197–198
Michigan
    Department of Corrections, 74–75, 79–80, 89–90
    incarceration rates, 121
    prison costs, 121
    State Police, 75
    truth in sentencing rules, 121
    Women's Commission, 79
Michigan for Families Against Mandatory Minimums, 121
Miller, Zell, 30
Minimum security prisons, 19, 149, 173–182
Minnesota Correctional Facility at Faribault, 161
Minority religions, 82–85
Modern Healthcare, 89, 97
Monshannon Valley Correctional Center, 128
Mullins, Luke, 173–182
Multiculturalism, 175–176

N

National Center for Institutions and Alternatives, 189

National Commission on Correctional Health Care, 92–93, 95
National Institute of Corrections (NIC), 69, 94, 155, 158–159
National Institute of Justice (NIJ), 194
Nelson, W.R., 198
New Jersey, 120
New York, 33, 41–42, 60
New York Times (newspaper), 37, 44, 53, 55, 61, 169
Newton Correctional Facility, 84
NIC (National Institute of Corrections), 69, 94, 158–159
Nichols, Terry, 187
NIJ (National Institute of Justice), 194
No Escape: Male Rape in US Prisons (HRW report), 65–66
Nolan, Patrick, 83–84
Non-violent criminals, 23, 31, 44, 116
Nutraloaf, 103–107

O

Obama, Barack, 44–45
Oshkosh Correctional Institution, 155
Overcrowding, 31, 115–125, 118
Oz (television), 72

P

Pack, Bob, 119
Paris, Joseph, 93–94
Parkland Health & Hospital System, 91
Parole
    elimination, 168–172

inmate performance, 165–166
no-parole policies, 168–170
older prisoners, 170–172
recidivism rates, 170
The Sentencing Project, 169
states, 164–172
Parsell, T.J., 65, 67–68, 72
Pell grants, 36
Pennsylvania
  Department of Corrections,
    124, 127
  George W. Hill Correctional
    Facility, 133, 138
  House Bill 1469, 126
  inmate health care, 160
  inmate population, 127
  Monshannon Valley Correc-
    tional Center, 128
  Philadelphia Prison System,
    139
  prison costs, 127–128
  prison privatization, 126–128,
    131–132
  State Correctional Institution
    at Laurel Highlands, 161
Pennsylvania Prison Society, 146
Pennsylvania System, 16–17
Perdue, Sonny, 30
Perzel, John, 137
PetSmart, 207
Pew Center on the States, 22, 46,
  50–51, 120
PFM (Prison Fellowship
  Ministries), 172
Philadelphia Daily News, 133, 144
Philadelphia Prison System, 139
Plessinger, Gretl, 142
PLRA (Prison Litigation Reform
  Act), 86–88, 125
Political prisoners, 16

Politics, politicians, 23, 27, 44–45,
  53–54, 116
Porro, Alfred, 173–176, 178–179
Prison camps, 173–182
Prison Fellowship Ministries
  (PFM), 172
Prison Litigation Reform Act
  (PLRA), 86–88, 125
Prison politics, 100
Prison Rape Elimination Act
  (PREA), 66–67, 69–71
Prison Trained K-9 Companion
  Program, 202, 205, 208
Prisoners, prisoner rights, 18
  aging, 127, 148, 155–163
  Eighth Amendment, 26, 57,
    91, 103–104, 190
  First Amendment, 84
  healthcare, 89–97
  legal standing, 86–88
  women, 19, 36, 59–64, 60
  See also civil rights; inmate
    lawsuits
Prison-industrial complex, 27, 37,
  42–43, 89
Private Corrections Institute, 135
Privatization, private prisons, 27,
  115–116, 123
  Arizona Department of Cor-
    rections, 130
  Beaver County, 138
  Bureau of Justice Assistance
    study, 130
  contracts, 129
  Correctional Corporation of
    America, 170–171
  correctional healthcare, 135–
    137
  Delaware County, 133–139
  GEO Group, 133–139

George W. Hill Correctional Facility, 133, 138
legal safeguards, 129
lost jobs, 131
nationally, 127–128
performance, 129
proponents *vs.* critics, 135
Reason Foundation, 131
types, 126
Urban Institute study, 130
Project for Older Prisoners, 156
Public opinion, 18, 22–23, 192
Public safety, 42–43
Punishment, 19–20

R

Race relations, 44–45, 63–64, 98–102, 175–176
Reason Foundation, 131
Recidivism, 36–37, 40–41, 49–50, 170
Rehabilitation, 18–19, 26, 149
Reilly, John, 134
Religion, 82–85, 172
Religious Freedom Restoration Act (RFRA), 82, 85
Religious Land Use and Institutionalized Persons Act (RLUIPA), 82–83, 85
Reynolds, Mike, 47
Rhode Island, 118, 120
Richburg, Keith, 117–121
Ritter, Bob, 82–85
Riverside Correctional Facility, 67
Ross, Jeffrey, 183–192
Roth, Rachel, 59–64
Runner, George, 48
Runner report, 50–51
Russia, 36

S

Safley, Turner v., 82
San Francisco Chronicle (newspaper), 98
San Francisco VA Medical Center, 159
San Quentin State Prison, 98
Saunders, Debra, 47–52
Schevitz, Tanya, 98–102
Schniper, Mathew, 200–209
Schwartzenegger, Arnold, 118, 123, 125
Scott Correctional Facility, 73, 78, 80
Second Chance Act, 37
SecureAlert, 146
Segregation, 98–102
Seidel, Jeff, 73–81
Sentencing, 35–37, 117, 168–170, 180–181, 189
The Sentencing Project, 117, 169, 180
Sexual assault, 65–81, 137
SHU (Special Handling Units), 183
Silverdale Detention Center, 130
Smithsonian.com, 16
Soering, Jens, 164–172
Solitary confinement, 18–19, 36
Sourcebook of Criminal Justice Statistics, 176, 182
Southern Center for Human Rights, 33, 86
Sowell, Thomas, 53–55
Special Handling Units (SHU), 183
State Corrections Officers Association, 131

State prisons, penitentiaries, 53, 139
    costs, 25, 39, 120–121
    early release programs, 117–118
    Eastern State Penitentiary, 16–17
    elderly prisoners, 156–163
    healthcare costs, 94
    privatization, 127–132
    state mandates, 99
Statistics, 22, 34, 36, 55
Stemple, Laura, 66–67
Stevens, Debi, 201, 203–204, 207
Stewart, Julie, 181
Stop Prisoner Rape, 68, 72
Struckman-Johnson, Cindy, 67–68, 70
Supermax prisons, 19, 26, 28, 149
    confinement conditions, 187–190
    costs, 191
    downsides, 191
    Eighth Amendment, 190
    future prospects, 191–192
    history, 183–185
    human rights, 190
    incarceration effects, 190–191
    incarceration rates, 187
    politics, legislation, 185–186
    proliferation, 185–187
    reporting, 184–185
    research, 184–185
Surdin, Ashley, 117–121

T

Taxpayers, 115–116
    private prisons, 126, 132–133
    state programs, 50, 74, 110–113
Taylor, Mark, 89–97

Tent prisons
    Florida, 140–143
    Maricopa County Jail, 108–110, 140–143
    prisoner advocates, 143
Territorial Correctional Facility, 200, 202
Texas Criminal Justice Policy Council, 158
Thomas, David, 157
Thompson, Dan, 122–125
Three strikes statutes, 23, 47–52, 124, 156
Tocqueville, Alexis de, 37
Trends, 148–149
Truth in sentencing, 121, 156, 168–170, 172
Turley, Jonathan, 156, 163
Turner v. Safley, 82
Two strikes statutes, 30–31, 156

U

United Kingdom (UK), 54–55
United Nations (UN), 26
United Nations Universal Declaration of Human Rights, 190
Urban Institute, 130, 190
U.S. Bureau of Prisons (BOP), 151, 193
U.S. Commission on Civil Rights, 82–83, 85
U.S. Department of Justice, 57, 79
U.S. Immigration and Customs Enforcement, 138
U.S. News (newspaper), 173

V

Van Zandt County, Texas Detention Center, 108

Vera Institute of Justice, 39
Victims, victimization, 44, 53
Violent Crime Control and Law
  Enforcement Act, 168
Virginia Department of Corrections, 165
Virginia Department of Criminal
  Justice Services, 169
Virginia-Pilot (newspaper), 172
Voting rights, 38

W

Wackenhut Corrections Corp.,
  133–139
Wainwright, Costello v., 141
Wall, Ashbel, 120

Wallace, Nicholas, 177
Washington Post (newspaper), 117
Werner, Richard, 193–199
Wicca, 85
Wicklund, Carl, 162–163
Will, George, 44–46
Wilson, James, 46
Women in prison
  elderly, 159
  incarceration rates, 60
  pregnancy, motherhood,
    60–64
  racial patterns, 64
  rights, 19, 36, 59–64

Y

Yousef, Ramzi, 189